Behind Our Therapy Doors

300 Plus Years of Clinical Mental Health Experience

Barbara Ann Newton

and

Kay Wilson Shurden

Editors

Parson's Porch Books

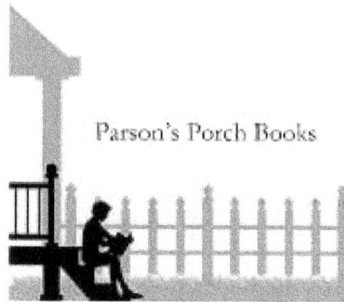

Behind our Therapy Doors: 300 Plus Years of Clinical Mental Health Experience
ISBN: Softcover 978-1-955581-80-6
Copyright © 2022 by Barbara Ann Newton and Kay Wilson Shurden, Editors.

Parson's Porch Books is an imprint of Parson's Porch *&* Company (PP*&*C) in Cleveland, Tennessee. PP*&*C is an innovative organization which raises money by publishing books of noted authors, representing all genres. Its face and voice is **David Russell Tullock** (dtullock@parsonsporch.com).

Parson's Porch *&* Company *turns books into bread & milk* by sharing its profits with the poor.

www.parsonsporch.com

Behind Our Therapy Doors

Abbreviations

CFLE – Certified Family Life Educator

CPCS – Certified Provider Credentialing Specialist

CTRTC – Choice Theory and Reality Therapy Certification

EdD – Doctor of Education

EMDR – Eye Movement Desensitization and Reprocessing

LPC – Licensed Professional Counselor

LMFT – Licensed Marriage and Family Therapist

LMSW – Licensed Master **Social** Worker

MBA – Master of Business Administration

MFT – Marriage and Family Therapist

PhD – Doctor of Philosophy

TF-CBT – Trauma-Focused Cognitive Behavioral Therapy

Contributors' Credentials

Gloria Smith Cissé, LPC, LMSW, CTRTC, CPCS
TF-CBT Certified Therapist
Choice Theory/Reality Therapy Faculty and Practicum Supervisor,
The Southern Center for Choice Theory, LLC

Ann Carol Daniel, LMFT, LPC
Clinical Member, American Association of Marriage and Family
Therapy
Member, Georgia Association of Marriage and Family Therapy
Member American Association of Pastoral Counselors
Approved Supervisor, American Association of Marriage and
Family Therapy

Sandra Hunt Gardner, LMFT, MBA
Director of Clinical Operations, Piedmont Behavioral Health
Masters in Marriage and Family Therapy, Mercer University School
of Medicine
Master's in Business Administration, Wesleyan College

Barbara Jo Koehnemann, LMFT
Certified IMAGO Relationship Therapist
Advanced IMAGO Clinician
BJK Therapy LLC

Nina M. Laltrello, LMFT, CAADC, CSAT-S, CMAT
Certified Clinical Advanced Alcohol and Drug Counselor
Certified Sex Addiction Therapist / Supervisor
CEO / Clinical Director, Relationship Recovery Center, LLC

Barbara Ann Newton, LMFT
Masters in Marriage and Family Therapy, Mercer University
EMDR Trained
B Newton Counseling, LLC

Sandy Shoemaker, PhD
Assistant Professor, Department of Psychiatry, Mercer University School of Medicine
Approved Supervisor, American Association of Marriage and Family Therapy, Retired
Licensed Clinical Social Worker, retired

Kay Wilson Shurden, EdD
Associate Professor, Department of Psychiatry, Mercer University School of Medicine, retired
Approved Supervisor, American Association of Marriage and Family Therapy, retired
Licensed Marriage and Family Therapist, retired

Andrea S. Meyer Stinson, PhD, LMFT
Associate Professor of Psychiatry and Behavioral Sciences
Associate Professor of Pediatrics
Department of Psychiatry and Behavioral Sciences
Mercer University School of Medicine

Kerri S. Thompson, LCSW
Certificate in Theology, The Southern Baptist Theological Seminary
Master of Social Work, The Carver School of Social Work, Southern Baptist Theological Seminary
Licensed Clinical Social Worker
Member, Clinical Social Work Association
Member, GA Society of Clinical Social

Betty Williams LMFT, MDiv
Doctor of Ministry, Spirituality Specialization
Masters in Marriage and Family Therapy, Mercer University School of Medicine

Dedications

You may notice several of the writers source Dr Kay Shurden as a teacher and mentor. Her friendship and inspiration were essential to the publication of this book. I am forever grateful to her, and I dedicate this book in her honor.

For You who have sometimes thought, "I should have been a therapist or at least I should have gone to one." It is not too late.

~Barbara Newton, LMFT

To women everywhere who want to make a difference, or as I told my children, make the world a better place for all.

~Kay Shurden, EdD

Contents

Introduction

You are holding in your hands over 300 years of clinical mental health experience. This rich resource gives you an inside look at how and why we practice the way we do. Twelve therapists were invited and gathered to write down how they found their way to the therapist's chair. You will learn how and why they chose this professional path. Their stories are as unique as the people they embody; racially, spiritually, chronologically and geographically. These stories may be an open door to encourage you to see one or become one too.

Every therapist has a back story. The beauty of the client/therapist relationship is that they are there for you 100%, like your elementary teachers that are there for you and they do not seem to have their own lives or concerns. When I had to leave a session once to have an appendectomy, I am sure that client was taken off guard and surprised that the therapist was attending to herself instead of him.

Our ages span across 45 years, and we are in different stages of our practices. Our licenses are varied. Some of us are working on new ventures and some of us have retired. We work in group practices, hospitals, universities and private practices. We are diverse culturally, spiritually, politically and professionally. Our paths have woven us together through professional connections, working side by side for years with our doors next to each other and clients that teach us that the important things in life deserve to be heard.

Coming Home… Again

Barbara Jo Koehnemann

It has been said we teach what we need to learn. The decision to become a relationship therapist had been percolating, inside me, long before entering the Marriage and Family Therapy program at Mercer University. By the time of graduation from the Master's level program, I was 49 years old, in my second marriage, with an adult son and a high-school-aged daughter. It was not my first rodeo. A co-owner in business, with experience in banking and television advertising sales, this would be at least my fourth career. It had been a long journey; it felt like coming home.

Being raised Catholic in the 50s and 60s, my self-image had been defined by the world around me. My entire community was Catholic: school, neighbors, playmates. It was a very close-knit, structured, ruled and sacramental upbringing, which meant it was both safe and unsafe depending on how you behaved. I have many fond memories of attending Holy Cross church and school, mixed with some confusion and disenchantment. Back then, attending any other religion's church was prohibited. Even reading the Bible was discouraged. The explanation was that we were not theologically educated enough to understand it and would need the interpretation of the priest so as not to misinterpret or misunderstand it. Although no longer a practicing Catholic, the foundation of spirituality of those formative years remains, and I value deeply my affiliation to the Daughters of Charity, a powerfully spiritual Catholic organization of women committed to the poor around the world. Yet, I have struggled.

Even as a little girl, I noticed that women were not allowed on the altar except to clean it. The sense of being excluded because of my gender was unsettling to me. Some of my thoughts were: why are women not allowed on the altar and why can't I be a priest? This seed of shame was planted at a very early and formative time in my life and took root and grew unbeknownst and unconsciously influencing some of the pitfalls along my path. It took years of trial and error and lots of getting back up and trying again to break through the rigid boundaries of those early teachings, while holding onto the universal principle of connection to a Higher Being. Becoming a therapist was one way that I broke some of my own barriers to actualize a part of my *priesthood* daydream.

One particular gender shaming memory from my early days was hearing that it was more important for boys in the family to go to college than it was for girls, reasoning that the boys would be the breadwinners and the girls would be at home raising the children. In my era, this was more common than not, and it instilled in me a discomforting feeling, a questioning that was squelched before it was allowed to form. A belief that to be *acceptable* meant denying questions of and discomfort with the wisdom of male superiority and authority, and it was proclaimed by church, teachers and parents.

As a sixth grader I remember an attempt to speak up against the norms of my environment. Catholic school was, for the most part, a very structured, uniformed and secure introduction to education, at least until the cracks began to appear. My teacher that year, Sr. Eugenia Marie, was an elderly nun who was a bit odd but seemingly harmless at first glance. She was strict and somewhat cranky and had some idiosyncrasies. In her classroom we kept hard tack candy in our desks, one of Sister's requirements in case of a nuclear bomb attack and the need for sustenance until we were rescued. My terrible sweet tooth was happy with that particular classroom requirement. If you have ever seen an old picture of kids hiding under their desks, practicing just in case of "the bomb," I was probably in it, another strange part of that year. Something that became clear was that it was unwise to disagree with Sister. One day on the topic of Sacramental Matrimony, a belief that marriage is meant only for procreation, I remember disagreeing with her, saying that "people did not get married just to have children; they married for love!" That was right before her face got red, and she started screaming at me. My recollections about that school year are slight, as I was often "sick" in order to stay home, far away from Sister's rages. Mercifully, my mother must have known how difficult my teacher was because she would relent and allow my feigned malaise. In the middle of the school year, poor Sister was carried out of the classroom by an emergency team. I was absent that day. Upon my return, there was a substitute teacher. I have often wondered how many parents and/or other teachers were aware of the strange behaviors of this sister long before it required medical intervention. So many things were put aside or swept under the rug. One did not question, make waves or leave because it felt like going up against God to do so.

Another young childhood experience that contributed to my shame about gender and sexuality was that my best friend and neighbor revealed to me that she was being sexually abused by her grandfather. Although she would not have used those words, she conveyed details that were incomprehensible to me. My vague and distant memory is that I told my mother about it, and it was not discussed again. In those days, there were subjects that were unapproachable, unutterable. Neighbors did not get involved in another neighbor's business. There were things that simply were not discussed. My friend and her brother spent a lot of time at my house with my family. In recent years, they have both thanked my mother for her attention and care of them when they were young. Today, my lifelong friend is one of the most successful people I know. She has told me that she spent a long time with more than one good therapist and was able to experience some healing. She is a resilient survivor.

My parents took me to a therapist, not long after this, when I was still in grade school. My fear of death was causing me difficulty sleeping. In looking back, it seems quite rational that there would have been a lot of fear connected to leaving girlhood. It could also have been transgenerational, connected to my father's losses of both of his parents before the age of 14. Or maybe it was just all the crazy stuff of life that was already all around me. After all, the 60's had arrived. So besides what was going in my church, school, and neighborhood there was the assassination of President Kennedy, as well as race riots and the Viet Nam War displayed on the black and white television screen each night. It's easy to see how fear or anxiety could be a psychological and emotional consequence for a sensitive child. The therapist wasn't too helpful. She told my parents it was

"Freudian," without explaining what she meant by that to me or my parents.

By my early teens, boys had become more interesting. Having 4 younger siblings, I often babysat them or watched them as they were playing outside. On one such occasion, I had walked down to the corner to talk to some neighborhood boys. Within a few minutes my dad's van turned the corner as he was coming home. By the look on his face, my expectation was to be punished, get scolded or be grounded. I did not expect the raging anger and physical violence that came out of my dad and at me that day. We never discussed that incident. My world shifted on that day, changing from being a girl who felt close to her father, to one who was cut off emotionally. The awareness of my irresponsible behavior could not overrule the anger of feeling betrayed and abused. It was decades later, through my training in brain chemistry, that I began to reconcile my dad's behavior as acting out of fear. This early cutoff became a regret, as he died before I was conscious enough to know what was needed to heal this rupture, which was more on my side than his. The ripple effect of this disconnection showed up in many ways. It has been an undercurrent in my difficulty in relationships throughout my life.

Psychology Today was first published in 1967. Reading the articles in it felt like listening to a familiar friend. They encouraged my interest in psychology and a desire to learn more about the field. There were two main currents running through my life in my teenage years. One was an interest in the combination of psychology and spirituality; the other was the desire to connect with the male gender. It was here that my life took a big detour. In reflection, two emotions arise: one is regret that I had to traverse so many rocky and uphill battles by my own doing, and the other is acceptance that this was my path and a necessary part of transformation. One thing that helped this process was learning that the limbic system is in charge much of the time, until about age 25, because the frontal lobes of the brain are not fully developed. At hearing this, I exhaled with understanding and a bit of relief. My teenage detours included some alcohol and marijuana experiments and some relationship auditions. By 19, I had experienced an unplanned pregnancy and a rebound marriage. It wasn't until after my father's death in 1992, by then in my second marriage, that I began to move toward becoming a therapist. Even though I had struggled through many ups and downs and been to two therapists by then, I had not yet been at the doorway of seeing myself as one.

After traveling to Arizona for my dad's funeral and burial, I returned home and two days later walked in the graduation ceremony for a bachelor's degree in Communication from Mercer University. At 40, in my second marriage, working and caring for a family, it had been a long and winding road to get to that stage both literally and figuratively. Fighting back tears through the entire ceremony, I was grieving many losses, some unconscious at the time. What I didn't know was that this grief was a doorway that would lead me home. In trying to heal my own grief, my closest friend and I began a ministry for the grieving at my church that continues today. It included a grief support group. In this support group, I experienced others' healing alongside my own. The experience became a passion and a training toward leading the group for over 10 years. It also fueled a desire to apply to the program at Mercer.

The journey through the program to licensure was like childbirth, a labor for sure and wonderful discoveries from some awesome teachers of wisdom. One of my personal favorites was Dr. Kay Shurden, with whom I had the honor of a one-on-one spirituality class. She helped me to explore my own spirituality and comprehend how I might bring it into my therapy sessions and/or simply let it guide my work. My admiration of and inspiration by this deacon in the Baptist church awakened an awareness of the limitations of my early church upbringing. She also encouraged an appreciation for its theological foundation and rituals that encourage the senses in transformation. Dr. Shurden opened my eyes to a more inclusive view of the spiritual world and helped me see that I would have made a good Baptist or Buddhist, or priest, or on any other path taken in the search for God. It is not so much the path but the desire and willingness that counts. She also introduced a way to see God as the Divine Feminine, expanding my ever-growing perception of The Creator, The God of My (very limited) Understanding. Dr. Shurden shared the poem "God Says Yes to Me," by Kalyn Haught, on a retreat. It is the essence of what she taught me. I hope you read it.

Post licensure and several life struggles led me to more new beginnings. These life experiences have been essential to honing my skills and sharpening my confidence in therapy practice. Through a devastating second divorce, a door to IMAGO Relationship Therapy was opened to me. Becoming certified in this therapy and integrating it became the focus of my practice over a decade ago. IMAGO is Latin for the word *image*. It represents the image we all carry of what love means; the messages we received, the memories we carry, the sensations and feelings that all together are held in that image within us. This includes both the positive and negative character traits of our early childhood caregivers. Even when the damage has been significant and new construction must take place for a relationship to remain connected, IMAGO Relationship Therapy can provide the tools toward that goal. In order to be most effective, each partner must bring their open, honest and conscious self to the process. The process requires acceptance and surrender. Surrendering the old ways and accepting the new. Accepting my part in the chaos and surrendering my defense mechanisms, these were the ways I used to protect myself in childhood. The challenge to grow into new ways of behaving in relationships that have been ingrained for many years can be both exciting and overwhelming. Being an IMAGO Relationship Therapist is the way I contribute to better relationships in the world. The single most satisfying aspect of my work is to help a couple deeply reconnect in a new way. I use this process for all relationships, from relationship with self to extended family relationships. I have seen families through reconnection after decades of cut-off from children and grandchildren. I have assisted couples after deciding to divorce, say goodbye in a way that helped them continue to take better care of their children as co-parents. And it has been my privilege to assist couples in crisis to find a renewed sense of joy and wholeness in the sacred space between them.

My couples' work is supportive, encouraging and structured. Structure is foundational. We need a place of support under us that feels trustworthy and firm. In this process, couples learn how to show up with openness and honesty and safety, with safety as the first step. I hold the space of safety for them until they are ready to hold it for themselves and each other. Just like parenting, it is my job to work myself out of a job.

There is one more piece of the puzzle that is primary to my focus in therapy: immersion into the 12 Steps through AA and Al Anon. Both sides of my extended family of origin have struggled with the effects of addiction and alcoholism. From my first AA meeting, I felt like I had come home. Finding recovery was an awakening that lifted me from the abyss of believing that the failures of my past are things to be ashamed of. The Twelve Steps have been instrumental in helping me understand the consequence of addiction and co-dependency on individuals, families and relationships. These two programs were direct paths to reconnecting with my core. Each one took a portion of my crookedness and smoothed out the wrinkles in the road. One of my favorite poems, "Please Come Home" by Jane Hooper, expresses the emotional connection to feeling at home. Easily found on the Internet, I hope you read it.

One gray day some years ago, I was bemoaning my history to one of my beloved colleagues, how I have a lot of nerve thinking I can actually help others with their lives with so many failures in my own. She said, "Well, you know what not to do." At first, I felt like saying, "That's not what I want on my bio!" The more I thought about it, the more I realized how all those pitfalls and suffering were my best teachers. There is a saying in AA to "not regret the past or wish to shut the door on it." There was a time when I hated that saying. I wanted to shut the door on the past because of shame. I wanted to hang onto the façade of *knowing* and doing things "right" and "winning." According to Brene' Brown, shame is a killer, a killer of resilience and energy and truth by way of any substance or distraction used to bolster the anti-shame appearance - anything to numb us from looking at ourselves: none of which work. All of which lead to more shame and destruction and disconnection. The reality is that all of that stuff in my past is the gold. It's not the successes or the "wins" that teach us the important lessons; the losses have much more to teach. The gem that I have to share comes from me mastering those losses. They are the things that shaped me into who I am and who I am shows up each week in the therapy room. Some really good therapists have taught me and walked with me and shown me how to grow through conflict, disappointment and grief. I want to be one of those people for others.

One of my favorite stories: One day a bright and cheerful man was walking along enjoying the sun, when suddenly he fell into a deep dark pit. He could not see anything or hear anyone. He was alone. He began to yell for help. Another man came along, heard him, and peeked down into the pit and said, "Don't worry, I have a ladder. I will go get it and come back." The man in the pit waited and waited; the man with the ladder did not come. He began calling out for help again, when a woman came along and looked down into the pit and said, "I will go and get help and come back." He waited and waited. She did not come back. Louder and more desperate the man started yelling for help again, when suddenly an old woman looked down into the pit and then jumped in. The man was startled, bewildered and angry and said, "What have you done? Have you lost your mind? Now we are both lost, and there is no one to get help!!!!" The woman calmly looked at him and said, "I've been here before, follow me, I know the way out."

Becoming the
"Story-Catching Change Agent"

Gloria Cisse

I am not simply a counselor. I am also a social worker. I am not only interested in the individual. I am also interested in the family and the systems that the family must live within. I do not want things to remain the same. If someone comes to therapy with me, I hope they get the change they want by the time we complete our work. As a result of what I have experienced—educationally, professionally, and personally—I feel I have become a "story-catching change agent."

What does this mean? While I strongly believe that what happens in the past cannot be changed but that we can work to undo some of the harm caused by the events of the past, I cannot ignore "the story." Listening to someone's story, for me, is like watching a movie being produced inside my mind. From the beginning, the story includes a person's earliest memories, how their parents played or did not play with them, how many moves the family made, how much food was available, the older people in their life, extended family members, divorces, and deaths. The story also includes what they believe is bringing them to therapy. Listening to their story and watching their face and body helps me to understand the real reason a person is sitting in front of me, not just the "cause" that brought them to treatment.

A series of events have led me to this place, starting with my own family experiences and my need for counseling and continuing through my undergraduate, graduate, volunteer, and career experiences. I have earned degrees in social work and mental health counseling from Fort Valley State University, a second master's in social work from the University of Georgia, and additional work toward credentialling in infant and childhood development. I have sought short courses and other ways of becoming educated. At the same time, I have had on-the-ground counseling and administrative experiences.

I recall the circumstances surrounding my decision to become a therapist. I was working toward my degree at UGA. I also was a licensed professional counselor and working with an advocacy organization. After completing my first graduate degree, I was unable to obtain a job in my field of mental health counseling without an advanced degree. However, I always felt that I was a social worker more than anything else. Plus, my mentors, who were both social workers, were telling me that there were so many more opportunities for advancement if I had the MSW. To obtain this degree, a practicum or internship was required. I searched, found, and was hired in my first "counseling" position at a foster care agency, providing services to children, a type of work I had not done before.

If you have never worked with young children in counseling, you will not fully appreciate the apprehension I felt when my first young client presented in my office. I had very few toys and no skills with which to use them if they did exist. I was determined to try my best not to cause any further harm to the young people who came into that room and sat with me. Because it was a foster care agency, the children who came to see me had experienced all kinds of traumatic events.

Bethany was a 7-year-old girl who came into foster care because of severe neglect and abuse. She was born into a family that struggled with substance abuse and poverty. Bethany was removed from her birth family because her mother and father had traded her young, innocent, fragile body for drugs. The first day she walked into my office, I was nervous. She looked as if she was ready to have a lot of fun. I did not know what I was doing. I presented her with some toys and sat in front of her as she played. I talked with her in the same manner that I had used with my grandchildren. (Yes, I was a grandmother by the time I began working as a therapist.) I asked her questions about her day and what she had learned in school. We were busy in this seemingly casual conversation when Bethany's entire demeaner changed. It was almost as if we had entered a movie. I was watching her play unfold like frames in a picture show, one at a time. She was looking past me, either not speaking or speaking very softly, picking up and replacing toys without looking at them. I was stunned, so I sat and watched her. After some time, she began to play normally again. She had disconnected from the room. I did not know what I had done to contribute to this situation. I thought I had caused her harm. I realized later that Bethany had experienced a dissociative moment in my office. If I was going to help her and children like her, I needed to learn about how trauma impacts the mind and body and then how to treat the traumatized child to the best of my ability. I saw in this girl many of the behaviors that I had seen in my own family. I had to do something different. Ironically, the entire time I was learning to work with traumatized children, I was working with adults who had committed sexual and physical violence against the people in their lives.

One of my sisters, Linita, had been working in a child advocacy center for a few years, and she was also a person I talked with about the plans I had for my life. I spoke with her about what I had witnessed, without giving identifiable details. She told me I lived in an area where there was a high need for therapists, specifically to work with children exposed to traumatic events.

I had been working in this agency with children who had experienced sometimes multiple traumatic events, but I did not know what to do with or for them. My lack of knowledge about treatment methods available for these children sent me on a search for treatment models. I found a trauma-focused, cognitive behavioral therapy training that was fully online. I attended a play therapy class at UGA. I found play therapy classes listed online, signed up for them, and traveled to whatever place I could afford to participate in those classes. I completed an online training that was facilitated/developed by Bruce Perry and read books by Bessel van Der Kolk, Peter Levine, and Babbette Rothschild. I quickly turned this training into action and used everything I learned with the children sitting in front of me. To my dismay, this led to a conversation with my immediate supervisor. She asked me what I was doing with the children, apparently because she saw that they were getting better. I told her that I thought helping the children get better was the ultimate goal of treatment. I did not last at that job; however, I did learn the importance of what it meant to practice within my scope of competence and other ethical standards.

I was transformed by my work with children and adults, hooked on becoming the best therapist I could be. When one technique or set of techniques did not appear to help my clients get the relief they desired, I searched for and offered others. I became comfortable sharing with my clients the fact that I might not be the "right" therapist for them, and if I was not, I would help them find another therapist.

Listening is one of the many techniques or tools to use in the process of healing through therapy is listening. I did not really understand the significance of this skill or how I used it in therapy until clients began to ask me, "How did you know that?" I had learned to listen with all of my senses without ever being aware that I was doing it. Indeed, I was learning to hear the entire story of a person's life and to see it through at least three lenses: trauma exposure, attachment, and choice theory. Significantly, I began to understand that hearing these stories told to me by the people who longed to be heard was not enough. Somehow, I had to hear the story, interpret the meaning of the story, summarize it into bites that could be given back to the client in such a way that they could tell that I was really listening, and then guide them through the creation of a plan leading to healing.

While working with Tracy, a consultant I am using to help me obtain an endorsement in infant mental health, I found out about the term "holding." Tracy has helped me tremendously. She asked me, "How did you learn about holding?" Of course, I needed her to tell me what that meant, and she did. This information helped to give a name to what I had been doing with people my entire life, but more importantly to what was happening when my clients told me their stories and I was able to hold their story long enough to help them create an effective plan for improving their mental health. This is a significant part of "story-catching." Listening to the story, watching body language and picturing the experiences of each individual helped me to connect with them in a very meaningful way. I have almost always been surprised when I understand something about a person's circumstances and tell them, and they exclaim, "How did you know that?" I say to them that they just told me, but they do not understand because they never really uttered the words that I was able to see and hear.

I found social work completely by accident. I, not unlike many other college students, changed my major several times. While attending Wesleyan College in Macon, Georgia as an undergraduate nontraditional student, I failed a class in applied physics. Crushed, I spoke with the department chair, and she helped me to see clearly that what I wanted in life was to help people, not be a medical doctor. I left that school and headed to Fort Valley State University (FVSU) to pursue a degree in sociology. That was the subject I thought would lead me to helping others. It turned out that FVSU did not have a major in sociology. I spent a couple of hours speaking with Terri Kulkosky, chair of the behavioral sciences department. Terri, my friend, and later Dr. Kulkosky suggested that I take a class in social work to see if it I had any interest in it. I was hooked! I knew that I was a social worker, and I could hardly wait for the next class.

I earned the BSW from FVSU and headed to Atlanta to work for the Georgia Coalition on Domestic Violence. What an amazing experience that was! I had an opportunity to work with one of the most interesting and intelligent Black women I have ever met. The director of that organization taught me a lot of valuable lessons. For instance, it does not matter how many people show up for a presentation; just do it with all your heart. She gave me an opportunity to put my education about social work and what I had learned in the domestic violence shelter to work for victims all around the state. We were able to obtain the first statewide proclamation declaring October as Domestic Violence Awareness month in Georgia. While I served as division director, I helped to facilitate the first billboards across the state that advertised the 800 number that rang into the nearest domestic violence shelter. I also arranged for domestic violence shelter staff across the state to obtain medical insurance through Blue Cross/Blue Shield. It was a wonderful time in my life. This work, along with the work I was able to do with victims, has set the stage for all of the work that I have done for my entire counseling career. I learned about advocacy and the importance of advocating for those less fortunate. I also learned that a person like me could not advance in the field without an advanced degree. There was more work for me to do beyond advocacy that required that I have an advanced degree. I still did not think that I wanted to be a therapist.

I cannot move on without talking about a case that was significant in shaping the way that I work with people who have experienced domestic violence. It was the first time that I had worked with a victim who had killed her perpetrator. Hearing this woman's story, listening to her cry—no, scream—as she recounted her story, holding her hand, sitting with her in court, understanding what happened to her children, caused me to know that I had to do something. And I did. I returned home, applied to FVSU's mental health counseling program, and earned my MS degree. I was still not convinced that I wanted to become a counselor, but at least I had the credentials to do it.

During the time that I was completing my undergraduate course work, I was introduced to many theories and counseling techniques, but reality therapy stood out for me through a book written by Gerald Corey. Reality therapy fit my personality. I felt at home with this theory because it allows the therapist to be directive, not to tell people what to do, but to compassionately place the responsibility of a person's mental health in their lap. The theory also teaches that individuals have some ability to control their mental health, which excited me to no end. If it is possible to teach people that they have some control over their mental health and they are not simply actors in this wonderful game of life (mental health), then we can change the game. No longer will people who seek counseling feel they are at the mercy of the therapist or medication—they can do something to improve themselves. Since William Glasser developed and published information about reality therapy in the 1950s and 1960s, much of what was written in the textbooks referred to reality therapy. (Glasser published his book on choice theory in 1998, and this concept did not make the textbooks before I completed my undergraduate degree.)

I did not see a "formal" means of learning to practice reality therapy until I had completed both of my master's degrees and started working at FVSU in the counseling program. I still remember the day that a friend of mine, Jeri Crowell, brought an advertisement to the counseling center to see if anyone there wanted to respond to it. When I saw what it said, that the Glasser Scholars program was accepting applications for counselors to participate, I could hardly contain myself. They were looking for counselors working in universities who wanted to learn about choice theory and reality therapy. Sixteen people from around the world were chosen to participate in the program, and I was one of them! What an amazing experience it turned out to be. Not only did I learn about choice theory and reality therapy from Robert Wubbolding, John Brickell, and Maggie Bolton, but I also received my certification in Edinburgh, Scotland. It was inspiring to watch people from all over the world, practitioners of choice theory/reality therapy, behave as if they were practicing the theory with each other. The certification was structured, but they used lead management techniques to guide us through the process. I had never experienced anything like this before.

I returned from Edinburgh excited to teach the world—at least the people I came into contact with—choice theory. All we do is behave, and the only person's behavior I can control is my own. We make choices all day long, and those choices are designed to meet one or more of our basic needs. Choice theory/reality therapy is not the only tool in my bag, but I think of it as my sharpest tool. One other thing I really like about choice theory is that the counselor can teach the theory to the person sitting across from them, when they are ready to receive the information.

I have also taken countless numbers of continuing education classes in play therapy, cognitive behavioral therapy, couples counseling, infant and early childhood mental health, parenting, human sexuality, etc. I am a trauma-focused, cognitive-behavioral-therapy-certified therapist. I am working to complete my endorsement in infant-early childhood mental health. I want to be ready for whatever is presented to me in the therapy room. I finally feel as if I can help people, a dream I have had since childhood —a dream deferred because of childhood sexual abuse, rape, domestic violence, a diagnosis of major depressive disorder, suicidal ideations, extreme poverty, homelessness, and systemic racism; a dream that I can finally hold in my arms the way that I hold the stories of my clients in briefly my heart.

I can teach anyone choice theory, but I can only teach therapists, counselors, and other mental health professionals reality therapy. This became the focus of the conversations I had with my daughter Andrea and my son-in-law Andreas as we were working to decide on a name for our new business. So, on October 10, 2010, we registered the name: The Southern Center for Choice Theory.

Prior to deciding to start a mental health practice, I had worked with Ronald Hughley, LCSW, at his practice for about 10 years. It had been a very good working relationship, and I had learned a great deal from Ron on how to provide services to adult sexual offenders, children and adolescents with sexual behavior problems, and family violence perpetrators. Early in 2010, Ron announced that he planned to stop doing counseling and offered me the part of his practice that centered on working with the offender populations. As owner of the Southern Center for Choice Theory, I took over all of the leases for spaces and sexual offender and family violence clients that were a part of Quality Directions, Inc. We obtained the licenses for products along with our business licenses in the counties where we had offices. I went from being a therapist in someone else's practice to managing team members at three locations. At first it was a huge challenge, and I am very happy that my daughter and son-in-law agreed to do most of the "business" stuff while I was responsible for the therapeutic side of the business.

In 2021, when we had been in business for about 10 years, we had the opportunity to become the lead agency in the Macon Mental Health Matters Initiative. What an opportunity! We were responsible for working with between 300 and 500 individuals in eight different communities across the county. This was the first year's goal. We partnered with several agencies to provide innovative therapies for the community.

I had been practicing counseling for some time when I realized who I was in the process and how to try to explain it to other people. I remember being asked about my niche. Initially, I was not sure what this meant. I had been working with individuals from ages 3 to 70-plus. I had worked with children who were traumatized by some life event(s), and adults who traumatized children and others. I worked with people who had "others" who came with them to therapy, and people who were mandated to therapy.

I cannot label myself or restrict myself. I am not only a practitioner of choice theory and reality therapy or TF-CBT or with adults or with children. I am both a counselor and a social worker. I am interested in the individual and also the family and the systems that the family must live within. If someone comes to therapy with me, I hope they get the change they want by the time we complete our work as I continue to try to be the "story-catching change agent."[2]

Gaye Ethridge, the social worker who was my counselor during a very dark time in my life, once said something during one of our sessions about me becoming a counselor. She heard and saw something that I did not. She planted a seed or perhaps watered a seed that was buried beneath the black, rich Georgia dirt. Regardless, I am now doing what I have always wanted to do: helping people have the lives they think they want to have.

I am still at the beginning of the work I plan to do with people in my community. I look forward to continuing this story about how to become a therapist, finding my niche, and helping as many people as I can.

A Circular Journey

Ann Carol Daniel

My journey into the therapy profession began in the small town of
Warsaw, North Carolina, at the age of two. The year was 1937. My
father was killed in an auto accident, and my 32-year-old mother
was left with four children under the age of 11. I was the
youngest, with three older brothers. I have no recollection of a
father.

Mother was a schoolteacher and, within the year, realized that she
was not able to efficiently   manage a large farm. The
encouragement of her family of origin led her to return to her
birthplace—Nashville, Georgia. She purchased a large home
across the street from her first cousin, Ellie Harvey. The Harvey
family became very influential and supportive in my life.

I was with my mother constantly and, on some level, I was aware
of her sadness. I recall at age five returning home from
kindergarten and falling up the steps of our home as I quickly tried
to get to my mother to show her the positive mark my teacher
had made on a picture I had colored. This was an example of how
I must have known that I was largely responsible for her joy. I
took this responsibility seriously until she died from cancer at age
49.

Mother was a very strong Christian. Her role in her large
extended family was one of spiritual guidance and wise
counseling. This was the only position left, as the other family
members were wealthy and held prestigious positions.

As the youngest child and as a female, I was shielded from many
of the struggles of our family and from the antics of my three
brothers. To be in the loop, I would frequently lean on the door
of my mother's bedroom as she prayed aloud. This was the
beginning of my learning confidentiality. I kept quiet.

I learned more about not discussing the problems of others, as my mother would not share with me when others had come to talk. When heavy wooden sliding doors would move across the tracks, I knew someone had come to confide in her.

Mother gave me her blessing. I was 11 years old, and after school, I met her at the First Baptist Church where she was in charge of the program for the Woman's Missionary Society. The church secretary informed Mother that Mrs. Crum would not be coming to give the fifth part of the program. As ladies began to gather, she cut the fifth part out of the printed program and told me to be prepared to read it. The meeting seemed very long, so I had more than 30 minutes to study. When it was my turn, I walked down to the lectern and recited the fifth part. I looked at my mother to be certain she was impressed, and she was tearful. After the other ladies left, she put her arm around me and said, "You can do anything you ever want to do." Her words have been my mantra for 75-plus years.

Mother realized that her income had to be increased, so she designated three large rooms to be rented as an apartment. I vividly recall 10 families with whom I was very connected and would eagerly listen to the stories of their journeys. These families, like O. Henry's stories, were woven into the fabric of my life.

As Shakespeare wrote: All the world's a stage, / And all the men and women merely players; / They have their exits and their entrances / And one man in his time plays many parts. These four lines from *As You Like It* describe the families in our apartment. I remember when the mother of an eight-month-old boy came bursting into our side of the house. She was hysterical in that her mother-in-law was coming to take her baby! A plan was quickly put into place. I was to exit the rear of the house and quickly carry the baby to a friend's house. I will never forget crossing our large backyard and fleeing quietly. (My maternal grandfather, a lawyer, later resolved this situation.) In therapy, as in life, some of the loudest messages you receive are never spoken. I learned from my mother, "What happens to the renters is their story to tell, not ours." And so, I never told this story.

The afternoon of my mother's funeral, her youngest sister, Frances Fuller, told me I was to live with her and her family. I packed my clothes and never returned to my house. The Fuller and Harvey families provided every need I had and also many luxuries. I was given, among many other gifts, an education at Tift College.

Mother had always instilled in the four of us how important an education was. My oldest brother Billy became an electrical engineer, my middle brother Jack became a geologist and taught at the University of Oklahoma, and my youngest brother Bobby became a pharmacist. Now it was my turn.

I graduated with a major in English and a minor in sociology and did my student teaching in Thomaston, Georgia. The State of Georgia awarded me a two-year scholarship to obtain a master's degree in counseling/social work. I was accepted at Columbia University in New York. I was "on the way". And then I met Billy Daniel!

Billy and I were engaged for a year, while I taught English at Irwin County High School. In a beautiful wedding ceremony, Dr. I.W. Bowen, my Tift College religion professor, officiated. Billy had built a new house during our engagement period, and I soon adjusted to living in Thomaston. I had chosen family over a master's degree. I added two more years to my teaching career and then chose to study interior design.

Billy and I were partners in so many areas. As a team, that involvement included sharing the same views in parenting our three children: Al, Marian, and Matt. It included a strong work ethic. We were striving for success as we helped with the goals of each other.

Since I was an interior designer and owner of Coach House Antiques, Billy and I made a trip to England to purchase authentic furnishings. Billy, who was a company commander in the National Guard, operated a large construction company with an asphalt plant and had a truck dealership. We remodeled rental properties. One of the most significant purchases was acreage on which Billy, Al, and Matt built a 23-acre lake. It is where we call home today.

In 1964 we purchased a large Greek Revival home in which to raise our family. For many years we worked tirelessly on remodeling the house while maintaining its integrity. In 2020 it was placed on the Georgia Register of Historic Places.

We were very active in the First Baptist Church where we were leaders of the youth, Billyserved as a deacon, and I taught Sunday School. Life was good!

Then, in 1981, Billy died at age 46.

I was overwhelmed with shock and grief. He had never missed work due to being sick. I thought that with the premature death of my parents my major griefs were over. The thought of educating and launching three children seemed impossible. (Yes, the three children did receive an education and get launched. Al graduated from North Georgia College, Marian received her undergraduate and graduate degrees from Wesleyan College, and Matt graduated from Berry College.) And then there were the businesses.

I knew if I was to survive, I must make a change. The logical step would have been to eliminate some responsibilities. Rather, I chose to add one more.

In November of 1982 I was involved in an asphalt paving job when the spreader broke. I thought that if I was going to do more than just survive, I had to occupy my mind in areas that were not business-related. I changed clothes and drove to Macon.

I had limited knowledge of Mercer University. I knew the hero of my childhood, my maternal grandfather, Judge Judson H. Gray, had graduated from Mercer's law school.

I met a congenial and helpful Jo Anna Watson who, after an inquiry about my interests, directed me to the office of Mary Ann Armour in the medical school. Mary Ann had just transferred from Auburn University and was in the process of starting a marriage and family therapy program at Mercer. I knew at that meeting that I would apply, and I knew my life would begin to change.

It was only during the return drive to Thomaston that I realized my life had gone full circle and I would be getting that master's degree in 1984 that I had turned down in 1957. I would complete a circular journey of 27 years that was as predictable and straight as an arrow; it just took a very circuitous route.

The pull to change my life was like an undertow. I was aware there was opposition from family and well-meaning friends. I worked during the day and attended classes at night. My older friend, Dorothy Hightower, would call each evening to check on my safe return to Thomaston I had entered another world that was a needed and welcomed diversion.

In August of 1984, having been a 49-year-old protégé of two encouraging and learned professors, Drs. Kay Shurden and Mary Ann Armour, I graduated with a master's degree in liberal studies and a concentration in marriage and family therapy. At that time there was no licensure in Georgia. In 1988, when Georgia began to require licensure, I was grandfathered in as a professional counselor. In 1990 I took the state boards and was also licensed as a marriage and family therapist. In 1999 I became an AAMFT-approved supervisor.

In 1984 I was named Woman of the Year in Upson County. I felt more robotic than woman, however. Those were difficult years as I sought to divest so many business responsibilities. In 1986, after operating an asphalt and grading business for five years, I sold all the equipment and maintained the property. I wanted to be more fully engaged in the practice of psychotherapy. I definitely felt this was my calling.

Through the years I have spoken at the Georgia Association of Marriage and Family Therapists (GAMFT) state conferences and presented workshops and seminars with other professionals. I also made a presentation at a pastors conference in which I described the work of a therapist in a church setting. (Remember: my mother told me I could do it.)

I have always maintained a private practice. The majority of referrals come from the medical profession, insurance companies, and previous clients. Frequently, I acknowledge to clients that some of them seek my help because I am very direct; on the other hand, others don't come because I am very direct. I do not deal with generalities. Regardless of why they've come, I am honored and humbled by each client who chooses to spend time and finances seeking help from me.

My initial work experience was in private practice in a doctor's building in Thomaston. I was ñ supervision with Mary Ann Armour, who was very clear that I needed to experience couples in therapy. My clients were primarily individuals, however. I strongly suggested to a client that she invite her husband to the next session. She came alone the next week and reported, "He brought me, but will not come in." With her permission, I went to the parking lot nearest my office entrance. A man was seated in a pickup truck. I encouraged him to come into the building (also the office of a gynecologist) since I was seeing his wife. He immediately rolled the window up and followed me into my office. I directed him to take the chair by my client. In a note of complete surprise, she said, "Who is he?" I had brought in a stranger whose wife was there to see the gynecologist. I was seriously trying!

The acceptance of therapy as a tool to help individuals and families through challenging times has advanced significantly. In 1984 my office was across the street from the hospital. Clients would frequently park their cars in the hospital parking lot and enter my office through a back door. Today, therapy is seen as a significant contribution to one's mental health. I believe most individuals can benefit from therapy; certainly, my family and I have.

In the winter of 1986, the opportunity came to join a group going to Oxford University to study with a certain professor. I was assigned to Michael Argyle, who was recognizedas the world' s authority on happiness. (I was not aware there was one!) On one of the coldest days London ever recorded, we were snowed in for hours at the university. Prior to meeting Dr. Argyle, I had read all his books. I asked him for a condensed version of his recommendation for happiness. He responded with "That is simple: it takes satisfaction in the workplace, belief in a higher power, and a significant individual in your life." I have found his words to be true but would add: Stay in the present and do not spend time wishing the past could have been different.

If I was to become a full-time therapist, I knew I needed to consider relocating. Macon was the appropriate location with its proximity to Thomaston, the programs at the medical school, and a group of friends, most of whom were therapists. It was time to move; I was a grief-bearer in Thomaston, and I felt the pressure to stay in that role.

My family and friends opposed my desire to move. On moving day, only Ellene Cook came with a quart of soup. My daughter Marian assisted with packing. In December 1987 the movers packed furnishings and memorable oil paintings and followed my car out the driveway. When I reached the first red light, I thought to myself, *I cannot do this.* I put my hand on the door handle, intending to get out of the car and tell the movers we must go back—and then the light turned green. This still remains one of the most courageous decisions I ever made.

In my therapy practice I feel it's important for my office to be a comfortable and well-appointed space, both for myself and for my clients. The room is spacious, and lamps provide adequate lighting. The majority of the furnishings are representative of my years as an interior designer. The high ceilings allow space for an antique, nine-foot Gothic bookcase that serves as a convenient library. I am "at home" in this space with individuals or groups, and I sense my clients are also comfortable.

To provide additional physical and emotional security, I ask clients to lock the door as we enter. In the foyer, instrumental music plays, creating an additional sound barrier. Spring water is available. My administrative assistant greets clients and assists with intake and insurance issues.

Where clients choose to sit is significant, especially couples and families. For example, an eight-year-old directed her parents where to sit on the sofa and quickly sat between them. She crossed her legs, looked directly at me, and asked, "What do you want to know?" I replied, "I already have obtained important information."

My primary goal as a therapist is to be a good listener. I listen intently, without judging. This concentrated attention helps me respond effectively and frequently. To ensure that my response is correct and that I am hearing well, I have, on occasion, done a role reversal with the client.

As a helper of others, I am committed to my own growth. I learn continually from reading, clients, and professional seminars. I seek to model the behavior I wish my clients to achieve. For example, I try to maintain good mental and physical health and a high level of energy. I am never bored, as each client and each story is different. When clients enter my office, they have made the boldest of statements: "I have come for help." I genuinely care for those who seek my help. When I am aware that my own experience in a given area may be helpful to a client, I willingly share.

Since the advent of family therapy in the early 1950s, it has increasingly grown as a concept to help individuals and families during difficult times. There are many theoretical approaches that are useful in therapy, but of all the theories available, I believe that family systems therapy holds the possibility of more lasting change. I use it as a guide, but the theory is not central; the client is. Family systems therapy allows for creativity and spontaneity in helping clients meet their goals. Together we explore several options that may help them solve their problems more effectively than the direct and rigid ones they might have initially considered.

As I endeavor to help clients shift their expectations from me to themselves, my major goals are to help clients understand themselves, move toward constructive problem-solving, and take the world of therapy out into the real world where they will apply this process to what they may encounter in the future.

It was Murray Bowen in 1957 who presented reports on his research using families with the patient. In 1978 he published *Family Therapy in Clinical Practice*, a textbook that included the major concepts of projection, family emotional processes, scale of differentiation, triangles, emotional cut-offs, and the generation transmission process. It is the Bible for systemic therapists.

To gather information from the generations of a client, a genogram is used. In thousands of clients, I have never had one that I did not initially get this information. This graphic family tree traces the family through three or more generations, showing the significant or major events that characterize the family. It frequently provides a gestalt of family traits and allows the therapist to see that the presenting problem may have the family as its source. (In training, I wrote about the Jimmy Carter family; the genogram provided evidence that the Carters conceived a baby when they were away from Miss Lillian.)

The genogram is a quick way to obtain a family assessment. It provides a way for the therapist to join the family as information is being gathered. Frequently, it evokes stories associated with the drawing of symbols denoting marriages, deaths, divorces, birth order, addictions, diagnoses, and relationships. Genograms are done in the first session and become a reference of pertinent information for the length of therapy. They provide an excellent introduction to family systems therapy and enhance the bonding process between client and therapist. If there is no bonding nor acceptance, no therapy takes place.

As a therapist, it is essential that I have a clear understanding of ethnicity, culture, religion, sexual preference, socioeconomic status, values, and belief systems. It is important to find a common ground and to be nonjudgmental.

Occasionally I am asked, "In what way do you see the therapy working?" One of the clearest examples is the significant changes that can take place if an individual can look with some objectivity at their family of origin and identify the positive traits (work ethics, honesty, resilience, etc.) and the negative traits (addictions, poor communication, lack of boundaries, etc.). Then to have the strength to leave the negative and continue the positive—and pass the positive traits to future generations—is one of the most significant changes that ever takes place. The family systems model is very helpful in achieving this. One of the many works of the therapist is to restructure the relationships that cause the dysfunction and to change what nourishes these symptoms.

Once I was helping a farmer-client work on some family system issues. I said, "To do this will be as difficult as hoeing a row of cotton." Two weeks later he returned and asked, "Where is the hoe?" We continued to work.

A therapist is bound by many rules of ethics. A very important one is never to have a dual relationship with a client. I do not go to the home of a client, but at the request of various families, I have been to the intensive care unit of the hospital, spoken at a client's funeral, and visited a jail. I have even gone to a hospital nursery to visit a couple who, after experiencing eight years of infertility, called and asked: "Please come see our baby boy!"

The systems approach can identify the respect or the disrespect of boundaries. If everyone's boundaries were respected, I would not have a client. There would not be sexual, physical, or emotional abuse, theft, affairs, lack of privacy, answering for another, or manipulations. Systems therapy is reminiscent of my entering the lives of the families who rented my family's apartment through my early years. I think this may be one of the reasons I am comfortable with systems therapy.

From 1988 to 2004 I worked every Tuesday at the Atlanta office of the Georgia Baptist Medical Center and at the First Baptist Church of Griffin. (Mary Ann Armour, in semi-retirement, used my Macon office on those days.) My pastor and friend, Edwin

Cliburn, had encouraged the director of the program, Gerald Jenkins, to hire me. Those were valuable years of professional growth. I trained under the psychiatric wing of Dr. Albert Davis, and we continue to refer clients to each other.

One of the many advantages of my years as a therapist is having attended many conferences—from San Francisco to New York—and having heard from the greats in the field of systems therapy. How rewarding it was to be present when Murray Bowen spoke and to be present with Norma Walsh, Bill Nichols, Craig Everett, Lyman Wynn, and our own Kay Shurden and Mary Ann Armour.

I do not see my past professions and experiences as something that currently define me. Rather, I see them as that which has been preparation for my work as a psychotherapist. The diversity of my life has provided many experiences that have served me well in practice. Alfred Lord Tennyson wrote, "I am a part of all that I have met." The part of me that culminated in being a therapist represents all that I have ever encountered. With the passage of time and with my experiences of therapy, I am grateful for the difficulties and the major events of my life. They have helped me do my best work and prepared me for being a therapist who could listen to the client's information and use it to help facilitate change—something we all need.

While in a session with clients, I frequently realize that I am also in therapy. Oftentimes, when they are putting salve on their wounds, some of that salve gets on me.

I am a person of hope and faith, and the possibility of helping another find hope in the most difficult of circumstances is both challenging and rewarding. We have met on sacred ground.

In 1990 I was searching for a unique gift to give my three brothers for Christmas. Calling on my draftsman experience in interior design, I began sketching the floor plan of the house in which we grew up. I began to cite events in each area that we would all recall. I became tearful and aware of what a therapeutic tool this was for me and would be for others. I was unaware how many memories I had repressed. I began to use this exercise with clients and found it very effective in uncovering and resolving many issues.

I made a presentation about this therapy approach at a workshop and Florence Kaslow, an editor who represented a publishing company, asked my permission to send me a book contract. I was honored, but never willing to take time away from my therapy practice to write a book. Perhaps the opportunity to write a chapter in this present volume will be sufficient. I am hopeful that, in a variety of ways, this "book" will encourage the reader to consider going to therapy or entering the field professionally.

As my therapy practice continued, an awareness came that I had experienced so many of life's difficulties and that this firsthand knowledge could be helpful as I worked with clients. These difficulties included being reared in a single-parent home and being a single parent myself, experiencing the business world, launching children, premature deaths, a distant child, and the single life. Dr. Frank Pittman, an Atlanta psychiatrist with whom I had family and individual therapy, said, "We come to this profession from our own need."

There have been many times when humor was a part of a session. In my third session with a precocious 10-year-old male, I said, "You know, talking to you is like talking to an adult." He replied, "I feel the same way about you."

When Lee Bowen became the director of the Mercer Medicine MFMT program, he was instrumental in securing many interesting programs. He brought in David Schnarch, the nation's leading sex therapist, to conduct a seminar. Dr. Bowen asked Max Kennedy and me to be dinner guests with him and Dr. Schnarch. Max and I were unaware that this was an audition.

The next day we were on stage as a sexually frustrated couple. This probably resulted in a comedy rather than a learning experience for the attendees. It was memorable. I recall the laughter on stage and in the audience. Dr. Schnarch had to deviate from his usual agenda due to the problems of the couple! Nevertheless, he offered us a role as traveling actors with him. (I knew Mother wouldn't approve, so I declined.) Through the following years, I sent couples to the Colorado retreat of Dr. Schnarch. Sadly, Dr. Schnarch died in 2020. His book, *The Sexual Crucible*, will remain a textbook source.

In 1988 Ella Mae Shearon conducted psychodrama workshops primarily in Germany, but Dr. Armour brought her to Mercer for all who wanted to learn these interventions. She was a master of creativity and taught the intervention of role reversals, demonstrating the open family and the closed one, having grave visitations, and creating dramas of the client. More than 30 years later, I am still using many of Dr. Shearon's effective techniques.

In 1988 I had a private practice at the Coliseum Hospital in Macon with Dr. Allison Grant. In 1991 I moved into the psychiatric center and had a private practice while sharing a building with three psychiatrists: Dr. Ray McCard, Dr. Dwight Bearden, and Dr. Stephen Mallory.

Practicing as a psychotherapist with thousands of families over a period of almost 40 years has been the most humbling experience of my life. To have the opportunity to accompany others on their life's journey is rewarding and purposeful. I believe therapy is effective, or I would not continue to carry a full load and be seated at my desk in my late 80s.

Several years ago, the director of Mercer's MFT program expressed appreciation for my referring seven (or more) students who graduated from the program. The one of whom I am most proud is my oldest granddaughter, Madison Baugh of the class of 2020. The circular journey continues.

In My Therapy Chair: Finding Myself and Finding a Passion for Helping Others

Sandra Gardner

My therapy chair is a traveling chair. It's been in the room with children, adults, and families. It has traveled countless miles with foster and adopted kids through foster homes, family homes, group homes, and court rooms. My therapy chair loves to bring people into the field and develop and mentor them. My therapy chair thrives on bringing calm to chaos.

I didn't know what I wanted to be when I grew up. The truth is, I am glad that I didn't. How can we find our way without a journey to help us get there? My involvement in the gifted program at Valley High School led to me securing a senior year internship in the emergency room at Presbyterian's flagship hospital in the heart of Albuquerque, New Mexico. It was exciting, it was chaotic, and I loved it. A medical assistant position opened up but with one big problem: The only shift was overnight on Thursdays, and I had high school classes the next morning. I begged my father to let me take the job. He never wanted me working during school because he was forced to work while in school to make ends meet, and it prevented him from finishing school. Eventually he agreed and I took the job. I saw a dead body for the first time: a patient who came in for cardiac arrest and didn't make it. It turned out he was the uncle of one of my classmates; I ran into this classmate as he was running into the emergency room, and I was wheeling a patient out. I couldn't tell him that his uncle was dead. I had to clean up the body and the room. What a sobering experience, an introduction into the complexities of real life. Maybe I would be a hospital administrator? My hospital experiences continued while attending college in Massachusetts. I worked in several Boston-area hospitals, Massachusetts General and Brigham and Women's. What an amazing time in my life, but the start of my college years still had not answered the question of what I wanted to do with my life. Little did I know, through a unique series of events, the path to my therapy chair was about to be revealed as I found myself in Macon, Georgia attending my mother's alma mater—Wesleyan College.

I moved to Macon at the age of 21 because of a boy I had met at my parents' 25th wedding anniversary celebration when I was 15 years old. He and I became pen pals and wrote letters on and off, and then two years after moving to Macon we married. While working multiple jobs and attending college, I began volunteering at the Methodist Home for Children and Youth as a big sister. After a year of volunteering, I desperately wanted to work there. I felt drawn to that type of work. At the time, I worked at a law firm during the day as my full-time job, waited tables in the evenings during the week, and was now working the night shift in a cottage at the Methodist Home on weekends. I loved it so much, I accepted a full-time live-in childcare counselor job and began working my way up the ladder. This is when the journey to my therapy chair truly began.

Looking back, what was I thinking? I was living in a cottage with 10–12 little boys, driving them around in a 15-passenger van, and working around the clock. I was only 22 years old, took a significant pay cut, and on top of all that decided to get married. Shortly after marrying, my husband moved in with me, all of the boys, and one huge mass of chaos. We lived in an "apartment" in the cottage, which was actually just a single room and tiny bathroom.

I developed a specialty working with boys with sexual behavior problems. The STARS program, which I helped develop, was incredible. A residential program for boys under the age of 12 with sexual behavior problems, it focused mainly on re-education. Some came from sexualized environments, and many were from abusive or neglectful situations. Most were removed from their parents by the State, and many had attachment issues. It was essential that the therapy and milieu were closely aligned. The program consisted of a critical mix of individual and group therapy, milieu of daily living, family therapy, and a solid plan for quality continuum of care after they graduated from the program and returned home or to an adoptive home or to another placement. Our program allowed me to train with Toni Cavanagh Johnson, one of the nation's leading experts on sexualized children, and to work with many remarkable kids, families, staff members, and mentors.

Jill Chambers Myers took a chance on me and gave me an opportunity; for that, I forever will be grateful. During my 24 years at the Methodist Home, I was extremely fortunate to have been mentored by Jill, Steve Rumford, Jeff Lawrence, Rick Lanford, Edwin Chase, Toni Roberts, Staci Fonseca, and Alison Evans. The professional growth I experienced under my mentors in turn allowed me to mentor and work alongside many tremendous people. Through the years, having been part of the development and careers of so many remarkable, passionate, and caring caregivers and therapists has been truly amazing. Most importantly, I am humbled to have had a part in the lives of so many troubled kids who are now mature adults raising their own families and being productive members of our world. I have such good memories of children and staff. The work in my therapy chair has shown me that you can overcome and move to a new place in life. Your past does not define your future. My 24 years at the Methodist Home directly contributed to the therapy chair I sit into this day. I am proud of the work I did, and I am proud of my commitment to advancing through education.

School was a major focus for much of my time at the Methodist Home. Working full-time and going to school made earning my degrees a much longer process than for most people. Over those many years, I would go on to achieve three degrees: a BA in Spanish from Wesleyan College, an MFT from Mercer University, and an MBA from Wesleyan College. I loved the classroom, the camaraderie with classmates, and the learning environment. I enjoyed the blend of clinical work and administrative/business management that has allowed my work as a mentor and leader for employees. My classroom time prepared me very well for life in my therapy chair; it did not, however, teach me to duck!

There are many memorable stories from my time at the Methodist Home, but some more so than others. In my early days I was trying to de-escalate an angry boy who proceeded to hurl a rock at someone. Unfortunately for me, his aim was bad, and his rock hit me in the head (I wasn't the one he was mad at). I saw red. As the pain and my anger built, it took a lot to resist the urge to run after him. It was an early lesson on de-escalation skills and not personalizing the acting-out of abused, abandoned, hurting kids who were apart from their families. It was also a great lesson in not personalizing the feelings or behavior of any therapy client. It's not every therapist whose clients throw rocks at them. Another time, while driving down the road by myself with 12 boys, a melee broke out. I careened into a driveway and pulled the instigator out of the van. As I was wrestling with him in the driveway, a very concerned homeowner called the police. Thank goodness, everyone was easily convinced that I was not abusing or trying to abduct a child. There was never a dull moment! And then there are the stories that truly stand out and remind me that I had indeed chosen the right path. I worked with "Jason" in the STARS program. He was special, smart, sweet, and had a lot to offer the world. After he completed the program and moved on to finish growing up, he joined the Marines. Some years later I was interviewing another boy, "Brandon," who had been living with his adoptive family but needed treatment for sexualized behaviors. This boy's older brother was Jason, the one I had worked with years prior. The freckle-faced, blonde-headed boys were biological siblings, but had been separated when they were removed from their parents. When Jason was talking to the adoptive mother about the struggles of Brandon, he pulled my business card out of his wallet and told her to contact me to get the help his little brother needed. I had worked with the older brother and then his younger brother, many years apart. I knew I was right where I was supposed to be.

I was not only the therapist and social worker, but I also supervised the staff and the program. I worked all hours. One night, while tucking in a 6-year-old boy, and after many nights of tucking him in and telling him "I love you," he stared at me blankly. I realized that he didn't know what that meant. Can you imagine growing up in an environment where no one told you they loved you, especially as a child? I faced the challenge of undoing that neglect. How could I make up for that? How could I teach those essential, foundational lessons after the development was done? In Erik Erikson's Stages of

Psychosocial Development, by the time most of those kids got to us, they had already surpassed the stages of Trust vs. Mistrust (Hope), Autonomy vs. Shame (Will Power), and Initiative vs. Guilt (Purpose). We had a big job!

It was easy in my early years to feel anger toward the parents who neglected these children. While some parents made a conscious, willful decision to harm their children, most were lacking the skills to parent as they should. I developed an understanding of the family systems that created the children and families I worked with. I was able to have empathetic awareness and relationship and use that and rapport to work to change the system. Most of our kids still loved their parents, and most of them wanted to live with their parents despite the fact they were abused, neglected, or not well cared for. That is what they knew, and it was just the way it was. It was my job to challenge the deficiencies, teach new skills, and build a healthy system. I did not mind the therapeutically messy cases. I liked the challenging parents/families. Put me in a room with intense family conflict and drama, and I was right where I belonged. What a feat to win in that environment! It was about respect, genuine care, honesty, and challenging people to think differently and grow. I had to join with people to truly create change.

In-home therapy was a big part of my job. I spent countless hours traveling the main roads and back roads of Georgia. I had lots of good memories—and different kinds of music—on those long road trips. I still get a smile thinking about one of my boys learning to appreciate Louis Armstrong on those drives. I even got out of some speeding tickets after sharing my story/purpose for the trip. I tried so hard to love those boys and fill the void they had experienced. It was important to understand where the child came from, where the child was returning to, and to build a rapport with the family to gain their trust. I was a guest in their home but had to understand the dysfunction and talk about hard things with them so the child could return, do things differently, succeed, and remain in the home. I never knew what type of environment I might be walking into; I had to be humble, accepting, and accommodating. One of my protégés, an up-and-coming therapist and leader who I was teaching to take over my program, was hesitant to take drink/food/gum from a family. I insisted she accept what was offered, because something so simple was very important in building rapport and trust so that she could then say the hard stuff to them and have them receive it. In those days I was therapist, social worker, friend, and surrogate mother/parent—as were all of the therapists at the Methodist Home. They were an amazingly dedicated group who gave their all and went above and beyond. I am incredibly fortunate to have worked with them.

In my therapy career I've benefited from various mentors, of whom Kay Shurden was most significant. I first knew her as a professor and advisor at Mercer Medical School's program for marriage and family therapy. I continued my relationship with her in supervision for my professional license and in therapy. She helped me make the hardest decision of my personal life in therapy—which led to a very good outcome. Our class gave her a caricature as a graduation gift: she was an owl, our wise mentor. My other professor mentors were Sandy Shoemaker, Steve Livingston, Melton Strozier, and Lee Bowen. As students, we were in therapy ourselves. I remember when I asked my therapist, Diane Hall Smith, a rather embarrassing and I thought mortifying question. She laughed, completely normalized my fear, and we moved right on; she had a way of making things okay. My fellow students in my MFT program and licensure group supervision process were Carol Mathias Gorman, Barbara Koehnemann, and Barbara Newton.

My career growth at the Methodist Home continued to evolve, and I became the regional director for its Macon campus and clinical director for its therapy and outpatient services. When the Home opened a new campus in Columbus, Georgia, I helped start and develop a program for sexually abused kids. I began to work with adults whose children had been removed from them by the State. This was a new challenge. Many of the children involved were foster kids or kids whose families were never on the radar of state social services and therefore had experienced childhoods without full nurturing and guidance. Many of the moms and dads were losing their children through termination of parental rights. I stood by their side while they either won their fight to regain custody of their children or lost their fight and lost their kids forever. There's a lot of honor in helping mothers and fathers to accept losing their children forever and helping them figure out how to go on with life after that trauma—maybe even the transition to a future with more children or a new family. Transition is always a challenge.

When my time at the Methodist Home ended and I transitioned into a new job, with less of a direct therapy role, it was hard. But when you have chosen the right path for your life's journey, the universe has a funny way of reminding you just at the right moment. Recently, at my current job, I was approached by a woman who worked at the hospital. She said, "I saw your (curly) hair and thought that was you," and we embraced each other. She was a former client and told me about her new family, her new son. We talked about the four children she lost. There's a lot of honor and dignity in helping someone process the loss of their children and still move on with life. How many of us could lose our children, possibly never see them again, and still function—still go to work, still have a relationship, still have a regular life, not completely lose it all and give up? To care for and therapeutically love someone in that position is truly honorable. It's about respect, genuine care, honesty, and challenging people to grow. It's why I will always love my therapy chair.

A pivotal point in my life that helped to deepen what I had to offer as a therapist came when I experienced personal tragedy. My father died unexpectedly, and I had a late-term pregnancy loss after years of infertility treatments and trying to have a baby—both within a week. I'd had a rather ordinary childhood/upbringing—fairly normal and uneventful—which is good except that I didn't have emotional strife to draw on, to identify with people who were hurt or hurting, to really understand their pain. I didn't know what I was missing. I didn't know the depth I lacked in my emotional make-up. After my losses, it changed me, it deepened what I was able to feel, appreciate, and identify with. My favorite quote from the brilliant author/researcher/social worker, Brene Brown, is "The dark does not destroy the light; it defines it. It's our fear of the dark that casts our joy into the shadows." For what I learned from my darkness, I am thankful, and I believe it has benefitted those I work with, those in my therapy chair. And it deepened the relationship I have with the staff and therapists I have been privileged to mentor. It reminds me why I will always love my therapy chair.

Currently, I work with inpatient and outpatient behavioral health in a hospital setting. It was a difficult decision to change jobs, but an endeavor I couldn't turn down. This has been a tremendous opportunity to learn about addiction/chemical dependency, partial hospitalization and intensive outpatient levels of care, electroconvulsive therapy/ECT, and more about working with adults. The intricate workings of corporate healthcare and the complexities of a hospital system have been a challenging and fascinating (and sometimes vexing) learning experience. I got to see echolalia (repetitious speech) in person for the first time. It happens to be the very same hospital where my husband, an inpatient clinical pharmacist, works. How inevitable to come full circle to my teenage musings to work in hospital administration.

There's nothing fancy or elaborate about my therapy style. My practice has been guided by the basic principles of my life be genuine and caring, be honest, and be trustworthy. Life is about love and friendship, figuring out difficulties, helping others who do not or did not have these things readily available to them, or maybe just temporarily lost them. My style's basic origins are systemic therapy (patterns across systems) and cognitive behavioral therapy (thoughts, feelings, behaviors, common sense). The therapist-patient relationship/alliance is essential. I'm a proponent of mindfulness by nonjudgmentally helping clients be aware of their current state, but my style must also be adaptive/eclectic/transient—depending on the type of client and situation. I adhere to certain key tenets:

Respect – I seek to treat everyone with common decency and respect.

Directness – I say what I mean and in a way that people will hear but try first to build a relationship with them so they can trust me and receive it well.

Challenge – I think differently, do things differently, step outside my comfort zone, and take a chance.

Hands on – I'm willing to do the work and "get my hands dirty."

Multitasking – I have a specialty in multitasking.

Optimism – I am an eternal optimist, though sometimes to a fault in that I don't quickly sniff out when a client is doing something they shouldn't be doing.

Pay Attention and Stay Open to the Journey

Nina M. Laltrello

My route to becoming a therapist in my mid-30s was a very circuitous one. I didn't know about the field of psychology or therapy as a profession until 9th grade while sitting in the back of psychology class during what was my study hall period.

I spent my first 12 years on the barrier islands of southern New Jersey. Then we left our close-knit, extended Italian family and moved to Atlanta because my father wanted better opportunities for work. The move to Atlanta was upsetting but took on more of a quality of adventure. I settled in, made great friends, and easily adapted to our new life in the South.

After a few years in Atlanta, my father was offered another rung higher on the corporate ladder climb. That step involved relocating in 1977 to Germantown, a suburb of Memphis. Knowing our move from New Jersey to Atlanta went well, I looked forward to the move to Germantown with an open mind and eager anticipation—until I started school. The adjustments to the town and school were very hard. I felt like an outcast invading and had difficulty breaking in. Moving in the middle of the school year did not help the cause, nor did the fact that some of my classes did not transfer from Georgia's school system to Tennessee's offerings. Not knowing where to put me in the middle of the semester led me to sitting in the back of the psychology class that captured my interest.

Being a good student, I buried myself in my studies. Germantown High School was a college prep school. Its slogan was "Best of the Preps." The grading system was rigorous: 95-100 equaled an "A" grade; 88-94 was a "B." I had been an "A" student most of my life, so this bar was a little higher to reach for those top grades. For lack of a social life, my study life filled my afterschool hours.

One had to have permission to take Mrs. Deaderick's AP Psychology and AP World History classes. That first semester at Germantown High School I was given a bird's eye view to her psychology course. I was fascinated learning about Sigmund Freud and Carl Gustav Jung and how one could predict human behaviors based on knowledge about personality and brain function. Mrs. Deaderick treated her students like adults and prompted fascinating intellectual discussions based on a synthesis of ideas and the materials students were expected to read. Psychology was not a regurgitation of vocabulary and theories in the textbook. Mrs. Deaderick assigned cutting-edge books about people in the human condition, social justice issues, and feminist studies. *The Grapes of Wrath*, *The Women's Room*, and *Looking for Mr. Goodbar* were on the list of more than 20 books from which students were to pick five and apply psychological principles, character analysis, and theoretical constructs from the psychology textbook and vocabulary words learned.

I came to my study hall period that semester entrenched in the topics discussed but was not allowed to enter discussion as I was not technically in the class. I couldn't read the textbook, but I could learn the vocabulary and theories from the class discussion. I took notes rather than use the time for my own study hall. Freud's personality theory was fascinating to me and led me to read many books about him as the father of psychology. I did get a copy of the class reading list and began to read the books on that list over the next few years. They were fascinating and thought-provoking. I couldn't wait to be a senior so I could take the class officially and join in the discussions.

My parents knew I was not happy with our move and the difficulty I felt fitting in at Germantown High School (GHS). Shortly after getting settled in school, an opportunity came up for students to travel to France with the Greater Memphis French Club. It was a long shot, but I asked my parents if we could find out more information and if I might go. I held a 100 average in my French I class. I loved my teacher, and I loved learning the language. My godmother was born and raised in France. I loved her accent, and the idea I might be able to converse with her in her native language.

My parents allowed me to travel to France during that spring break in April following our arrival. They thought it would be a good idea to help me get more involved with people at the school. I could hardly believe I was going to Paris, France for eight days. Additionally, I would spend my 15th birthday in Paris! It was an amazing time. We were allowed to go all over the city without chaperones if we had two other students with us. I became very close with my roommate Melissa, a junior at GHS. We were allowed to stay out until a 2:00 a.m. curfew. We went to the most famous disco on the Champs Elysée and were allowed to have wine with our dinners, as the French do with their families. We had to speak French as best we could at all times. And we even got school credit for the experience if we wrote a five-page paper documenting our experiences and impressions. The trip allowed for so much fun, so much independence, and school credit to boot!!

That trip colored my language experience and spurned me to continue to take as much French as I could in my remaining high school years and in my college years. It also gave me a rich understanding of world history when I could take Mrs. Deadrick's AP class. As if Mrs. Deadrick was not making the class interesting enough, I had visited many of the areas that came alive in my mind's eye as I looked at the pages of my history book.

The French trip was helpful for meeting a few friends and having a little better experience at Germantown, but I really missed Atlanta and my friends there. So, as I began preparation for college and registering for the ACT and SAT tests, I began to realize that I could get back to Atlanta by going to college there. Also, somewhere in the 10th grade it occurred to me that I could take classes for credit instead of study halls and have enough credits to graduate by the end of 11th grade. I could get accepted to a college in Atlanta and return there a whole year earlier. We weren't allowed to take a full load of classes without a study hall, but I signed up for all classes and no one stopped me. I never asked permission, and the guidance staff was not aware of the plan I hatched in my head to get out of school a year early. (This was way before computers might have caught the overload registration.)

I did realize that if I skipped my senior year, I would not be able to take Mrs. Deadrick's AP Psychology class. We had to have permission to take the class, and it was very rare that one was given permission as a junior due to the mature subject matter. My grades were good enough that I was permitted to take her class, however.

Finally, I could sit in the psychology class as a student. All the materials, books, textbooks, and discussions were afforded to me. I was in blissful heaven. I loved it even more than when I was first exposed to it in 9th grade. I loved applying the vocabulary of the text to the very mature books we were reading. I loved the character analysis through the lens of psychological principles and theories. I loved learning about social justice and women's issues. Mrs. Deadrick expanded our world lens, opened our minds, and deepened our understanding of ourselves through her assignments. One of my favorite assignments was making a collage of who we were. I really learned a lot about myself by cutting images and pictures from magazines and other media to pictorially represent who I was at that time. Mrs. Deadrick would hold our collages up to the class and encourage students to guess who prepared it. We could own the collage as ours or remain anonymous.

I remember Mrs. Deadrick saying, "If you like learning these psychological principles and theories, and you like applying them to the situations and characters of the books, you might like working in the field of psychology." What? This fascination with understanding concepts and applying them to people could be a job--one you get paid for? Mrs. Deadrick's statement took me out of the classroom and into a daydream of wondering how one could do that for their life's profession. It was a crystalizing moment that captured my thinking about a career. I was excited to consider that as an option. I had been struggling about a major in college. This held potential. I had always excelled at, and loved math, and was wondering what I could do with math as a profession. Psychology was a foreign thought and a new consideration on my radar.

I could not see at the time how important the experiences of my traumatic move would shift my life focus and pave the way for a rich tapestry backdrop to my life's journey. I loved that psychology class so much. And I loved Mrs. Deadrick's AP World History class. These two subjects, along with my passion for France and the French language, would become pervasive themes that shaped the landscape of my interests and opportunities for my adult life.

At the end of my junior year, I showed up at the counselor's office to verify that I would have enough credits to graduate. I was one credit short! Senior English was missing in my credits, so I signed up to take it in summer school. In August of that year I earned my high school diploma.

During my junior year, my father decided to leave his job to start his own company and to move his operations and the family back to Atlanta. He brought me into his confidence for every detail in starting his corporation. He wanted me to know how to form a corporation, the strategies involved, assembling officers, legal papers, corporate charters, staff etc. I found it interesting. In our talks he hoped that someday I would want to be part of the businesses he was creating. From the time I graduated in August until I started college in January, we had almost daily meetings and conversations.

Sometime near the end of 11th grade as I finalized my college applications, I shared with my father that I was interested in majoring in psychology. I was shocked by what words came next: "You can't do that!" He went on to say that I had to find a major that would help me get a job, be successful, and make money to support myself. "You can't do anything with a four-year degree in psychology without going to school for the rest of your life! Our people did not come to this country for you to go to school for the rest of your life!! And who would want to pay you for listening to them? That is what a priest is for, and people don't have to pay money for them to listen!"

Well, I hadn't expected that. I don't think I knew enough to argue anything to the contrary. My father was wise and successful, and he had come from a long line of successful entrepreneurs and just thought I should be one too. Money was success in our family of Italian and Irish immigrants. I was sad, but did not have terribly strong feelings beyond disappointment and quandary for how I should redirect my thoughts for a major in college so I could become self-supporting.

We moved back to Atlanta in November of 1979. I was beyond excited to leave high school and Germantown behind and get on to the next phase of my life ahead of schedule. I was beginning to understand and take an interest in business developments and enrolled in Georgia State University's (GSU) College of Business.

I had no idea where to aim for a major. I was good in math, so I chose accounting. My accounting career was short-lived when I realized there wasn't much math beyond addition and subtraction. Information systems was a hot topic, and I was told that if you are good in math, you should look into that, and you could make a lot of money! So, I tried my hand with information systems. That too was short-lived; I tried passing that class three times before I gave up. Meanwhile, I took every psychology class I could as an elective. I loved my college introductory psychology class so much; I even brought my mom to class so she could meet the professor and see how interesting he was.

I was fully entrenched in business school and realized my dad was probably right about the inability to make any serious money with a four-year degree in psychology, so I decided to major in marketing. I realized it was actually psychological based: I loved the sales classes, and my "consumer behavior" class was the next best thing to personality theory class in the College of Arts and Sciences. I learned much about marketing, especially from two professors who were well known in the business world and who had a long-term impact on my life. I graduated from college in 1985 with a BBA—and a husband-to-be.

My business career took a very circuitous route. I had worked almost full-time through college at Food Giant grocery store. Within nine months of starting, I had been promoted to front-end manager. Throughout college I was making $10.30 an hour when the minimum wage was $3.10. It was a hard job to think about leaving, as most entry-level corporate jobs would pay far less.

My father's businesses were growing and expanding, and he continued to educate me about them. Occasionally I would help on a project or do consulting jobs to understand more about his corporations. At one point he owned wholly or in partnership eight different ones. He was a true visionary and had a real knack for seeing potential in utilizing computers and new technologies in the institutional food industry. He would share his wisdom and guidance: "You never want to work for someone else. And you never want to work in an environment that is dictated by the billable hour." I heard his words but would not truly understand the meaning and brilliance for years to come. My father was grooming me in hopes that I might take over his businesses one day.

Davis and I married in 1986, the year after he graduated from GSU. We both came from entrepreneurial, self-employed families with family businesses. Much of our relationship centered around school in the beginning and ultimately how we wanted to develop our careers and businesses. We were very supportive of each other's endeavors.

I would often take on consulting jobs to help food distributors automate their operations on technological platforms. This involved getting their "books of business" into a database format so that ordering, sales, and accounting functions could be mainstreamed automatically. While doing this consulting work, I maintained my job at Food Giant. I consulted and helped food distributors and other large institutions automate their operations. And I also became known in other industries outside my father's business circles. One such job led me to a full-time employment contract and ultimately a jump-start to my own business.

I converted an actuarial firm's data from an archaic database platform to another system that would work with the newest technologies. When I began my work, I had no idea what an actuarial firm did or what an actuary was but realized *that* is what I could have done with my math interests and skills. An actuary I met needed someone to run his new business; in exchange, he would help prepare me to become an actuary. With all the math I had in college, I already had the equivalent to sit for the fourth of seven exams. I was in heaven to find a way to apply my math knowledge to a career. That actuary and I formed a corporation and had a staff of seven people and marketed ourselves to the insurance industry of Georgia. Our business was very successful, so successful that my partner had other ideas how we would use our profits. It became clear that we had very different philosophical ideals about our corporation and such specifics as reinvesting, paying taxes, paying employees, and expansion.

Our differences caused me great stress. I was so stressed that I began losing sleep and having a lot of anxiety. My primary care doctor suggested counseling might be helpful and recommended a therapist. When I called to make an appointment, the therapist explained that her training called for bringing in "everyone around the problem." So, she asked my husband to come to "my session."

At my first session, as I was emptying my problems, I was just about to hyperventilate. The therapist artfully uncovered that my stress was related not only to my partner at work, but also to my partner at home. She discovered differing emotional styles, faulty communication styles, familial styles, and most stressful of all my feeling of failure if I left my business. I was feeling stuck, which escalated my anxiety. I would let my father down and all the entrepreneurs' shoulders on which I stood.

A few other things happened in my larger family system at that time. My younger brothers had become college age, and my parents' marriage began to suffer. My youngest brother had begun college and said he was thinking about majoring in psychology. This really angered me. How could he declare a major in psychology when I was just about forbidden to do so?

This therapeutic process helped me examine the issues that created my stress. I began to prioritize my professional life. My husband and I worked on renegotiating our roles and improving communication in our relationship. I sold my business to my partner and took a less stressful job in the corporate world, doing pricing and analysis. I could go home at night and not worry about rent, payroll, undone projects, and employees. My father thought I had sold my soul to the devil by taking a job working for someone else.

I continued in therapy and gained greater understanding of the dynamics of my family of origin and my husband's, and the issues that impacted our relationship. I eventually had enough courage to differentiate and say out loud that I always had wanted to major in psychology. I lamented to my therapist that I had "made my bed in business, so I must lie in it." My therapist challenged me as to why, which led to deeper discussions about the messages I had received. Those messages were not covert: finishing my education with a four-year degree was a very overt message I got from my father. I was the first person on either side of my family to get a college degree. My family was not knowledgeable about higher education. My therapist challenged me to consider a career doing something that I have passion for. My husband acknowledged that I spent all my time reading about psychology and psychological thrillers, so why didn't I consider going back to school.

The thought of returning to school for a graduate education in a completely different field was exciting and scary all rolled into one. My corporate job was very boring. I joked that it was like working on an assembly line. I was used to having much more responsibility and action in my work. I decided to investigate going back to school. Since I would be paying for my education, I needed to be sure that I was not going to squander precious resources (money and my time). I researched different types of psychology programs, everything from Christian counseling to psychiatry. I visited graduate school counseling departments, ordered catalogs to look at the curriculum, and networked with professionals in the field. I asked my therapist for two professional colleagues' names and then asked each of them for two more names and so on to build a network of people in the field. I had a list of questions I asked those professionals:

I then enrolled in Georgia State University's Project Explore, a four-week program designed to help students aim toward careers with knowledge based on career testing, interest inventories, personality testing, and other assessments. A counselor and graduate psychology students administered a battery of tests, and then the counselor met with me to discuss the assessment instruments. Next, I participated in a group brainstorming session based on my time with the counselor and learning the results of my tests. The final week included a one-on-one counseling session to assimilate and wrap up the synthesis of information. That process was very helpful and affirming. The results revealed that I had the skills and interest and personality to be a counselor.

I started looking more closely at the degree programs with consideration for which avenue to venture professionally. Social work seemed to be the most marketable degree, but the curriculum did not excite me! Marriage and Family Therapy (MFT) seemed much more interesting, but there was not a program near where I lived. However, there were two programs two hours from where I lived. The Licensed Professional and Community Counseling programs were local and of interest, but again, the curriculum did not seem as exciting. I applied and was wait-listed for the social work program. I also applied to Mercer University's MFT program, which was tentatively scheduled to offer a second branch in the Atlanta area.

I was accepted to the Mercer program in the fall of 1993. Unfortunately, the school would not be able to offer the program in Atlanta at that time. I decided to accept my position anyway. I would drive back and forth (110 miles door-to-door) to Macon, sometimes 2-3 times a week for 2 ½ years while I worked almost full-time at my corporate job, and in my second year, added an internship for my school practicum. I don't know how I fit it all in, except that I was so excited and fascinated to steep myself in the knowledge, it didn't matter what I had to do! Sleep was the first thing to go. I would tape my classes and re-listen to them on my drive to and from Macon. This was prime study time and method. I practiced meditation to give my body rest when sleep was hard to come by.

I jokingly referred to my MFT program as the Montessori School of Higher Knowledge. I felt so supported in my program. I felt as if the professors nurtured us in who we were and supported us in researching our own interests. They encouraged us to think about using our research in the future for community education.

I chose my internship site based on two things. One, I wanted to do marital therapy. I chose Catholic Social Services because of the stigma against divorce in the Catholic religion, and I figured more people would present with marital problems and hopes of salvaging their marriage. Catholic Social Services also offered live-team supervision, which was cutting-edge training at that time. I would be in the room with clients while a team of clinicians and other students would be behind a mirror or in another room watching via live video. "The team" would call on a telephone into the therapy room with questions, comments, interventions to perform, thoughts about case conceptualization, or to ask the therapist to come in the other room for a brief consult. I enjoyed that training so much. Initially it was a little unnerving, but it afforded me light years of learning in a brief time.

Beginning in 1991, and during my graduate school years in 1993–1996, my husband and I began to travel to Europe with great regularity. Until then he had never been overseas. My graduate professor and co-director of the program, Lee Bowen, noticed I was traveling a lot overseas. He mentioned to me that he had a friend who directed a counseling program overseas and if I ever had interest in working abroad, he could put me in touch with his friend. Later, that friend gave a presentation at our school. My husband encouraged me to keep in touch and hold on to the information, saying "You never know, it could work one day."

In addition to my coursework, the MFT program required 500 face-to-face counseling hours for graduation. With my work schedule, it took me almost a year and a half to complete those required hours. My internship supervisor came to me after about a year and said: "I might not be able to finish supervising you. I will be leaving in a couple of months to marry, will be moving overseas. I will be marrying a person who oversees and directs a counseling program for American military stationed in Europe… If you ever want to work overseas, you have excellent training, and I could put you in touch with the people who administer the program." My internship supervisor, Bonny, was marrying the best friend of the co-director of my graduate school program—but they did not know each other. It was like a "God moment" in my mind. Bonny was able to finish my supervision, and I graduated in December 1995 with the distinction of Most Outstanding Student in Marriage and Family Therapy.

Going to graduate school almost cost me my relationship with my father. While he could not believe I would go to work in corporate America, he thought I was surely possessed by the devil to go back to school and doubly for the degree I pursued. Sadly, my parents divorced while I was in graduate school. I would learn so much about my family in my studies. Predictably, when I no longer was my father's confidant and I differentiated from my family and chose an independent career path, and my brothers were heading off for college, my parents' marriage could not withstand what I learned in graduate school as "The Empty Nest" and the second-highest time for divorce in our culture. My mom had sought counseling, but my father refused. I know now in hindsight that put greater strain on their marriage. My father even said to me after graduation, "I can't believe you are going through with this. Your profession cost me my marriage." I knew that wasn't true, but he believed it and his words stung. When my parents divorced, my father descended into alcoholism. I discovered though my own therapy that I had been an uneducated marriage therapist (parentified child and surrogate spouse) my whole life in a variety of ways to both of my parents. Their marriage could not continue without their children triangled in for stability.

I started going to professional luncheons and state conferences while I was in school. I heard that was a great place to network and keep your ear to the ground for job possibilities. I met and hit it off with the chapter chair for my region of the Georgia Association for Marriage and Family Therapy. She and another friend I met through those luncheons worked at Georgia Baptist Counseling Services. They told me how I might seek an employment opportunity, and I followed through on their advice. I needed a letter of reference, so I asked for one from my professors Lee Bowen and Kay Shurden. Dr. Shurden knew the director of the counseling center at Georgia

Baptist Hospital, and I was hired shortly after graduation. I discovered it was a small world in counseling circles in Georgia!

I continued my corporate job for three years while I built my counseling caseload and worked toward becoming fully licensed in the State of Georgia. My husband and I also continued our regular trips to Europe. Around the time I became licensed we were heading to Germany. My supervisor, Bonny, told me she would be attending a conference there with her husband's program and that some of the state-side directors would be there also. She asked if I would like to have an informal preliminary interview for the program. I was surprised but jumped at the opportunity. I enjoyed meeting everyone assembled for the conference and learning more about the scope of work from the counselors working in the program. From that moment a seed was planted that I could not let go. I became determined to take the opportunity to work abroad. My husband was open to all the information, but doing the work would be harder, and it required addiction credentials.

In graduate school one of my professors, Sandy Shoemaker, asked our class: "Who would be your worst client?" In other words, "Who do you not want to work with?" I *swore* I never wanted to work with addicts and men like my Uncle Joe—a womanizing, narcissistic, alcoholic who bordered on sociopathy. Addiction ran strongly in my mother's family and when my father descended into alcoholism, I thought it was an issue too close to home to work with. I realized I did have some direct experience and wisdom, so I decided to pursue the specific credentials needed.

Davis and I had become Francophiles in our travels by this time. We traveled often to France, and we both spoke the language. I interviewed with ASACS (Adolescent Substance Abuse Counseling Services) in the Department of Defense contracted by Scientific Applications International Corporation (my actual employer). There was a space open in the U.S. Air Force headquarters at Ramstein Air Base in Germany, near the French border. This was my dream position. In January 1999 I became a Certified Advanced Alcohol and Drug Counselor (CAADC) and began pursuing with serious determination the position to work overseas.

On June 6, 1999, Davis and I (with our 200 pounds of dogs named Boris and Sigmund) boarded a plane for our three-year adventure overseas. My brothers joked that Nina's moving to Germany on D-Day would take Europe by storm. It was an amazing time for us. We traveled every chance we had. Davis was able to work in his family business via the Internet and to review real estate contracts. It was a wonderful time for us to be abroad. The economy was good and the exchange rate excellent, as I got paid in American dollars. I would work Monday through Friday, and Davis would procure our reservations and destinations for each weekend.

I could hardly believe how everything had come together from my high school passions and interests. We were in France weekly and Paris every month. We could speak the language and lived 1½ hours away from the Maginot line and the major battlefields of World War I and II. On longer vacation times we would go to faraway places such as Egypt, Morocco, and Turkey.

As I worked in Germany with substance-abusing adolescents, I became aware how high-speed Internet was impacting adolescents and families. The overseas investigators (similar to the FBI for overseas military bases) showed up to obtain my records for a child on my caseload as she had been pulled into an "Internet sex ring" unbeknownst to her parents. She had been groomed by an online predator via webcam. Adults seeing me for marital work began complaining about their spouses' use of Internet pornography.

When I returned to the U.S. in 2002, I began to "sound the alarm" to clinicians and parents that allowing their children to be on unfiltered Internet was akin to letting them loose in the red-light district alone and unsupervised. Additionally, there was research beginning to circulate about how the Internet and technology had addictive qualities. I became aware that I needed more training about this process.

Pornography use was a common complaint in my couple's sessions. I needed tools to understand people's preoccupation with pornography and technology, and to help break down the denial of how bad a problem it was becoming in their lives. I became aware of a man named Patrick Carnes, a pioneer in the field of addiction and specifically "sexual addiction" and addiction interaction. I could see that people would get clean and sober from substances, but then other behaviors such as viewing pornography or unhealthy eating patterns would creep in.

Dr. Carnes had researched and created the protocols for sexual addiction. He had written 225 clinical articles and 25 clinical books on the subject. Yet, there was a dearth of information on treating the betrayed partner and the family system impacted by this addiction. I signed up for training to become a Certified Sex Addiction Therapist. Dr. Carnes shared with us that he would take 30 of us on a mentoring year if we had ideas on helping to further his field of study. I readily identified the information needed to treat the entire system and wanted to use the combination of my family training with my clinical addiction credentials to fill in the gaps of resources for hurting spouses and families.

In my first mentoring year I wrote a blog about the things I was learning and teaching to my clients. It was a beginning archive that I could point clients toward for information. Dr. Carnes encouraged me to speak on the topics I was writing about and to write a chapter about treating the spouse for his book *Clinical Management of Sex Addiction*. I also became aware of how to do good clinical treatment for the family system, that it necessitated a team approach to deliver the treatment protocols Dr. Carnes prescribed in his model. At the end of my first year of mentorship, the project was not complete, so Dr. Carnes agreed to take 16 of us on for another mentoring year!

In my second year I began building the conceptualization for a treatment center for sex addiction treatment. I changed my individual practice to create Relationship Recovery Center, LLC, and changed office locations. I needed space large enough to have the staff I envisioned to deliver treatment. I then began hiring staff to deliver team treatment in the way Dr. Carnes prescribed, including individual, marital, group, and family therapy in different stages. I was now using all of my education (business and clinical) for the creation of this center. I was blessed beyond belief for the people who appeared to become my staff. We currently are a team of six clinicians and two administrative people to support the clinical staff in two locations. And in that mentoring process I met two men who would become my lifelong friends and eventually business partners in additional centers that we would buy and practice management by long distance. We each have two of our own centers for the family treatment protocols (six locations total) across three states (Louisiana, Illinois, and Georgia) that we own independently of each other. Additionally, we bought into a practice together that has expanded to two locations in the State of Washington and are planning to expand to other locations.

Many of my clients are very similar to the clients I feared I didn't want to work with originally. While in graduate school, I didn't have the skills or the training to understand how to help them, nor had I done my own personal work that would allow me to be most effective in leading people through their own pain. I have great compassion for those who come to see me. Often their lives are in shatters. Secrets have been longstanding, and betrayals run deep in the marriages that have been impacted by addictions, infidelity, and compulsive behaviors. People feel relieved to know that we specialize in helping them get out of the darkest moments they could have never imagined in having their secret life revealed. One man said, "Coming to see Nina is like a really good Netflix series. I can't wait for the next episode to see what happens in my life! It is so much better now." A woman in one of my Betrayed Spouses groups said, "I hate this crisis to my marriage happened, but I like me better now!"

Dr. Carnes was a man my father could have never imagined existed in a "therapy world." Dr. Carnes helped me utilize all of my gifts as a clinician and a businessperson concurrently. I love my work and am never bored.

I have a friend of more than 30 years who calls me the "Queen of Spook." By that she means I have an intuitive knack for paying attention to occurrences when they appear in my life and operationalizing them. I believe we all have that knack if we pay attention. I have seen my life as a journey to pay attention to the "road signs" when they appear. Thankfully I have put many of them together, staying open to the journey and operationalizing the things I am passionate about.

(Postscript: Unfortunately, my father died at the age of 64 while in active addiction. He saw me become a therapist, but he died before I created my centers for family treatment. My mother is 79 and has 44 years of sobriety. I have seen the tragedy of dying in the disease of addiction and felt the benefits of recovery and its impact on families. In experiencing the tragedy and the triumphs, I am comfortable in sitting with people in any condition, wherever they may be, but I do know there is a way out!)

The Butterfly is My Spirit Animal

Barbara Newton

She was in my therapy office when I saw a shadow out of the corner of my eye. A quick flash from behind the bookcase to under the sofa where she was sitting. Then I heard a rattle. With the appointment ending soon, I decided not to bring it to her attention. This was her final summary session to review progress she had made. I did not get her out fast enough. The squirrel darted near her feet into the middle of the room looking for a place to go. Not seeing any good options, it ran back under the sofa. Fortunately, this client was not in treatment for a rodent phobia which can be a real thing. She had a good sense of humor, and we laughed about it. I told the owner of our practice, who told her husband Bobby, who brought up some pecans and tried to lure the scared squirrel from under the skirted sofa. That did not work. Within an hour or two Bobby came back with reinforcements and a fishing net. The next time I went in my office the wall decorations were sideways, and the papers on my desk were scattered all over. I found some squirrel poop on the back of the sofa, and my bookcase was moved away from the wall. But the squirrel was moved down the street to a park, and my next client was ready for their session.

My mama said that at age six I was counseling relatives at family reunions. That must mean I am kind of a natural. As a young girl, I wanted to be a hairdresser—complete with conversation and sharing during the hair styling. Later I wanted to be a journalist, and then I just wanted to make enough money to have the things I wanted.

My trip from childhood to finding my work as a family therapist feels like a series of happy accidents. I was always more sure of what I did not want rather than having a clear vision or set path of what I did want. I would try things and learn what I did not want. It felt like the Robert Graves poem he titled Flying Crooked, when he writes, "You are a butterfly, not a crow. A crow flies straight to her destination. A

70

butterfly flies this way, then that, and still gets where she's going." I am always taking the side streets, looking in the store windows even if the sign says it is closed.

My parents met while working in an Air Force hospital when they were both active-duty airmen. Five out of the six members in my nuclear family are veterans. We moved almost every year when I was a kid. In my adult development class during college, I made little yellow Ryder moving trucks that I stuck on my life's storyline to show another change of residence. I had to make a lot of yellow trucks.

Straight from high school I stayed loyal to the family legacy of joining the military. While in the Air Force, I figured out that I did not want to make a career of working on C-130 airplanes in the Fort Walton Beach, Florida heat. The metal skin could burn right through cotton fatigues when I had to change an antenna on the top of the aircraft. So, I took my GI Bill benefit and went to college.

I started classes while on active duty and then continued after completing my four-year enlistment. I was married during that time and going to college was my job. I really liked college and was good at it. I had the time and energy to be interested in the subjects and to be creative with the projects. Being in school was a sweet spot for me. In my first psychology class the teacher asked, "Who is Barbara King?" After I raised my hand he said, "You earned 110 on our first test." It felt like something I could do well. I would never get a "B" again.

When my undergraduate diploma was mailed to my workplace in my new hometown after graduation, I opened it up and saw the words "Magna Cum Laude" printed on the document. Being the first in my family to attend college I had to look up its meaning in the dictionary because I had no idea what that was: "Mag-na cum lau-de. North American adverb. With great distinction (with reference to college degrees and diplomas)." I was not used to considering myself a high achiever. This was a good and strange surprise.

After I completed my degree in business, I decided to try for the only kind of work that I knew about that was stable with benefits. With a three-year marriage and a divorce behind me, I decided I needed to find a way to take care of myself. I applied for about 10 jobs with the State of Georgia. The first one I landed was as an accounting clerk at the probation office in Cordele, Georgia. I manually accepted fines, fees, and child support payments for a couple of years until there was an opening for a probation officer.

The week of the interviews the state auditor was going through my accounting books. Keeping financial records is not my best skill set. I would rather be tied to a tree than to sit in a chair all day working with numbers. I am sure the auditor went into the interviewing board and told them that it was in the best interest of the State of Georgia to get me out of those books and let me begin taking probationers to court and writing warrants. They listened to her, and I was promoted.

There I was in Cordele, Georgia, a small town with an exit on Interstate 75 between my hometown of Valdosta and the big city of Atlanta. I was rounding 30 years old, an active member of First Baptist Church, and needing to stay busy to stay out of trouble. I still had some GI Bill money left that I could earn by continuing my education, so I commuted an hour north to Macon and enrolled in graduate school at Mercer University part-time. I began this adventure in a criminal justice program in the University College evening and weekend classes. I did not have a special interest in criminal justice, but it was the field where I was working, so I went with it. This butterfly goes in the direction of something familiar.

I took one class and then was notified that the program had been discontinued, so I looked in the Mercer course catalogue and circled my finger until it fell on the marriage and family therapy program classes. I really can't recall how I decided to transfer to the MFT program. Perhaps a wise academic counselor swayed me in that direction to fill up the new program numbers.

I loved the classes. I didn't care that the classes went until 9 p.m. or that I was so busy reading and writing notes and going to supervision that the idea of reading a monthly decorating magazine was out of the question. The rest of the world fell away while I sauntered through my day job as a probation officer. I lived for the classes filled with stories of clients and treatments.

Early in my training to be a therapist, theories and new ideas swirled around my brain and heart in the therapy room. I would think to myself, "Oh, please, God: let me remember something I read or learned that can benefit this family." I had this crazy idea that I had to "do" something in session that was transforming, or I was not giving my clients their money's worth. I learned, however, that they just wanted to be heard. Simply being with them in the room while they processed their grief, worry, or fear was enough. Isn't that how it works with your friends? They sit with you and let you talk, and then they have their turn.

Some clients express regret at having to see a therapist over something they would have hoped a friend could help manage. We all don't have friends waiting in the wings to meet us weekly. My first guidance toward isolated clients, those who have not told anyone what is going on with them, is to give them the homework of having to tell one person about their situation before they come to the next session. It lifts the weight off their shoulders every time. The person they choose to tell is glad to know more and is supportive. We expand the system so the clients can feel stronger and not as distressed. Having the confidentiality is such a helpful part of treatment. Clients get this non-biased take on an extremely personal situation. Many of them describe the objectivity of a therapist as the most appreciated component in counseling.

During graduate school we were told to go to our own therapy to help us identify transference and to keep our personal issues out of our clients' therapy. With most of us juggling jobs and families and classes, it was hard to find time to add personal therapy sessions to our schedules—and most of us just didn't. All I had was a house, a job and a cat and still did not go to my own therapy. Required weekly sessions provided oversight where we would present our current cases to supervising therapists. In one of my sessions the supervisor asked me a question that hit a personal nerve. It caused me to ask,

"Who is getting the therapy here?" He answered, "I don't know. Who *is* getting the therapy here?" The next week all the students in my classes received letters to remind us to be in our own personal therapy while we were enrolled in the MFT program.

Having a clinical supervisor while working on a therapist's degree ensures that a new therapist provides quality care during the learning process. Students meet with their supervisors regularly, both in individual and group settings, to help manage treatment appropriateness. Not only are trainees learning theory by reading and taking classes, but they are also meeting with clients in the therapy room. Trainees need to be aware of any issues they themselves or clients may be dealing with that may present continuing challenges. For example, I worked with a colleague who did not take couples involved with online infidelity because that had been a personal stressor in her marriage. Often the therapist can work through the issue and bring that situation back to session after some time has passed. It is then that the counselor can offer laser insight that can benefit the client.

I continue to be thankful for my supervisors, Warren Jones, Mary Anne Armour, Kay Shurden and Lisa Mobley and the lessons I learned in their therapy rooms. During the time I was in supervision for my licensure, Mary Anne would come to my office on my lunch hour and meet with me and a few other therapists in training so that we could earn enough hours to become licensed. This time gift and her guiding us toward being good therapists was precious.

For many years I have continued to open my therapy sessions with client's by asking my go-to, solution-focused question: "What is your best hope for our meeting today?" Clients probably love this if they can take a moment and summarize the true intent of their having made an appointment. But they probably hate it if they are not feeling well and can't think straight, and especially if they don't know. Although my question can be irritating, it gives me a ton of information about a client's level of functioning and current ability to be self-aware. It also allows for some solution-focused questions to zero in on the immediate priority: Will you need a bandage? A tourniquet? An ambulance? We have 50 minutes to complete this investigation. I don't want to miss anything that might need to be addressed. Also, I often ask new clients about their previous therapies: "What was helpful to you?" The most frequent answer has been: "He listened to me, understood my situation, and he 'got' me."

What we focus on is up to the client, not me. I have had parents with six children come in and need to talk about their sister-in-law. I would have thought the stressor might be something with the kids. I once had an intake session with a young mom who listed some professional, physical, and marital issues as concerns. And then she laughed and added: "Oh, yes, and I should probably have told you that I am out of work and quarantined with Covid." I act as a guide, touring clients around the different areas they bring to my attention. I will listen and look for clues that direct me to areas that can be shifted for symptom relief.

Therapy content evolves. My sessions six months ago and six years ago look different. Early in my work I would have presented clients with a conglomerate of the last books I had read, the training I was interested in that year, and the focus I had on my life currently. In addition, the client would be getting myself—the entirety of my experiences, good and bad. There was me leaning up against the big redwood trees in California and me living in a domestic violence shelter for two weeks at age 20—the soup of my experiences with nature, adversity, victories, and the wisdom of lessons taught by former clients.

The listening and searching repeat at each session. We may be working on a specific issue, but clients come in with something that is screaming for resolution. This is the best kind of session for me, as it gives clients the opportunity to manage with the tools and new beliefs gained in earlier sessions. This will be proof of their ability to accomplish solutions on their own. Once they can do that, it won't be long before they feel better and leave my office for good. The goal is to get them back to what they enjoy doing.

I am writing this article during the winter of 2021 at what I pray is the height of the Covid-19 pandemic. Like most outpatient mental health providers, I had to transition to teletherapy in March 2020. In

Central Georgia we therapists have preferred face-to-face office sessions, although internationally and on the West Coast, providers have been using teletherapy for more than 15 years. Literally overnight my colleagues and I had to change the way we provide therapy to our clients. Most of us have been surprised at the ease with which this has happened.

I can't recall a therapist I have known that has left the field for a completely different line of work. It is surely a calling we are drawn toward. I have known counselors that have had to leave their agency or situation when it was an unhealthy environment, but they look for a new place doing the same genre of work. The happiest clinicians I have worked with evolve and find a new professional interest in mental health treatment every 5 years or so. The business evolves, new discoveries are still emerging, and opportunities are available to keep us energetic and curious. Sometimes they move toward the business side of the work becoming owners, teachers, professors or a combination of all of these. My evolution has looked something like this: interest and work in domestic violence, blended families, ADHD, ODD, working with children (when my own children were younger), anxiety and depression disorders, and my new favorite treatment, EMDR, which I will share more about later. And now, after losing the love of my life, I can see my future offerings including working with loss and grief. I see myself paying it forward and leading grief groups for people that have lost the loves of their lives, their children to violence, illness or suicide and the other losses we have. It will not be this year or next year, but it is on my calendar. I was able to attend a 12-week grief group at a local church. The leaders were patient, loving and had had their own losses. It made my transition back to living doable, and I am so thankful for their being willing to give their Sunday afternoons to attend to people they did not even know. They prayed for me and the others in my class. They gave us information that was practical about how to be on your own, how to get through holidays, take care of yourself and not be rushed through our grief.

An important change I've embraced in my practice is the use of EMDR (Eye Movement Desensitization Reprocessing). Initially, I put this treatment in the "hocus-pocus" category. I heard it was something about moving your eyes back and forth to help you feel better. Ten years later, I became aware of therapists referring their "stuck" clients to an EMDR therapist in a town north of me. The clients were often long-term, with multiple layers of classic traumas. After about six months, clients would return to their original therapist to continue making progress.

This treatment method sounded fast and effective—and I like fast and effective. EMDR had my attention. I put out my antenna for the people and training available. At about the same time, I had completed training to provide supervision for students working toward licensure. I liked the idea of being with students, using my experience and keeping up with modern practices, and I liked the idea of earning additional income doing something I would probably enjoy.

Even though I felt the need to use the investment of time and money that I had made in the supervision training, this EMDR method kept calling me. As I became more aware of the progress clients made, I fell in love with the hope of EMDR. I wrote an email to my colleague, Carol Mathias Gorman, LMFT, and told her about my dilemma. In two paragraphs I shared both my interest and investments in supervision training and the lure of the EMDR method, a practice that could provide relief and had possibilities. Carol's response was only a few sentences long. She told me to reread what I had written, and I would see it. One paragraph related to business and the other to passion. I had already made my choice to go with my passion, and it was clear in my email.

As I learned more about EMDR, the real benefit is that it can get clients unstuck if they are working in talk therapy and may have trauma blocking their progress. During the process of learning this modality, I became aware that a misunderstanding or an incorrect belief about oneself or another person or an anxious experience can traumatize the nervous system.

I am always surprised when a client agrees to try EMDR. I describe the treatment plan as this: "Together we will identify a negative belief you have about yourself. We will develop three targets to process past traumas. We will use bilateral stimulation such as eye movements going back and forth or a light bar that your eyes will follow back and forth. This experience will cause some things to happen." At this point I don't know what will happen or what this experience will be for the client. Sometimes the processing takes clients back to the trauma and lets them view it with their adult perspective. This allows for the beliefs to change if they felt they caused the trauma or if they need to give the responsibility to a perpetrator.

Sometimes the client's brain may choose to rewrite the story of their trauma. Abused children can visualize and feel themselves taking control of a situation and freeing themselves from the abuse. The client may process the abuser having consequences they may or may not have had in real life. The client may recall parts of the experience that were too difficult to remember at a younger age. Sometimes that remembering is helpful to gain insight into some adult not acting as they should have. They can remember a positive detail that makes the memory completely different than the way they interpreted it at the time it was happening.

Early in my work with EMDR I had a client working on a childhood memory. The processing took her to a 5th grade elementary classroom where she was watching a movie and the lights were out. A student behind her grabbed her breasts. My client told how she went to the teacher just as she had in school but was told: "Go sit back down and watch the movie now. You know he did not do that." When my client returned to her desk, the boy did the same thing again. Back up to the teacher she went but got the same disappointing response. And this is where my adult client began to rewrite her story. Instead of going back to her desk again, she walked to the door of her classroom and was met by her adult self. The student client and the adult client walked to the principal's office together to call her grandmother. The grandmother in the new narrative took the student home. My client had not remembered until the processing that both the student and the teacher got in trouble. And my personal favorite part was that boys who resembled her brothers scared the boy into saying he would not touch their sister again.

There is a warm, solid, dependable understanding of what happens when EMDR is finished—every time. Clients look different after they finish these sessions, as they sometimes do with other therapies. It is fascinating and an honor to sit with clients willing to go through the sessions and find their way to this good place.

***

I began writing this article by describing my wanderings through professional life, the butterfly that I am, getting lucky sometimes and missing opportunities other times. Kay Shurden had suggested a prompt to help us writers think about what to include in our chapters. She asked, "What did you say yes to along the way?" Thinking about what I said yes to makes me feel like I was in charge and in control of which way this butterfly flew. I said yes to the Air Force, yes to college, yes to being baptized, and yes to Ross Newton. I said yes to the marriage and family therapy program, yes to Kathy O'Neal, yes to Miona Gordon, and yes to gather clinicians together to write this book during a time when we could all benefit from having contact with each other. (Who can't benefit from a creative distraction during their first pandemic?)

I am 64 years old and want to keep working for about 10 more years. I like the idea of retirement, but I function better when I have structure and a schedule. Being a slow mover, I am just now hitting my stride and want to use my entire experience as a benefit to clients and myself. Fortunately, being a therapist can be done in many ways that suits our needs. I have worked full time, part time, taken extended time off for fun and out of need, worked at agencies with health benefits, agencies without when our family was covered by my husband's health insurance. I had the luxury of picking my children up from school most days which was important to me. Working from home during this pandemic has been such a relief. I have worked for myself in a private practice having virtual sessions from my home. This work as a therapist can be tailor made to suit your needs and desires as our lives change.

My hope as a therapist is to continue to work and stay interested in new therapy developments, like EMDR. I do not want to do any other kind of work, even if I have to deal with uninvited squirrels crashing my sessions. There is no doubt that I have found my calling and am leaning into the beauty of our match.

.

Saying Yes

Sandy Shoemaker

You may have heard the story of the newly licensed therapist who set up her practice in a small town. She took out an ad in the Yellow Pages and was surprised by the almost immediate influx of clients wishing to address sexual issues. Wanting to provide the best possible therapy for her clients, she attended conferences, enrolled in additional coursework at a local university, read voraciously, and sought supervision. Clients referred others, and word spread until she became somewhat of a local expert on sexual problems.

One day out of curiosity she looked up her listing in the phone book to discover she'd unknowingly been advertised as a "Sex Therapist." She laughed when she realized she had developed her niche quite by chance.

I love this story. Though I can't claim expert status, it is my story—all the more poignant because I almost missed becoming a therapist altogether (twice).

While working in a residential treatment center in the late 80s I asked our clinical chaplain to recommend a good therapist. "Go see Kay Shurden," he said. So I made an appointment, checked in, and took a seat in the lobby. Thirty minutes later I approached the front desk to ask if there were a problem. The receptionist informed me that Dr. Shurden was not there, and I would need to reschedule. Feeling irritated and a little full of myself, I said, "I don't think so" and left.

Kay called me that afternoon. She shared that she had had a family emergency and hoped I would reschedule. Hesitating only a moment, I weighed righteous indignation against getting help. Saying yes to Kay Shurden changed the trajectory of my life.

I sought Kay's help because I did not like my mother. I did not think this was okay but did not know what to do about it. Kay recommended I sit with my mother and look over picture albums of her life as a girl and a young adult. By doing so, I learned about her as the person she was before she became my mother. When she told me she almost didn't graduate from high school because growing up in Hawaii she never wore shoes, which were required for the graduation ceremony, I started to like her immensely.

Expanding on the genogram work Kay had begun was an intimate experience for my mother and me. She warmed to the process, and each story was a catalyst for more revelation. I began to admire this woman. Later I wanted to emulate her. She was to live another 10 years, which gave us time to enjoy a deeper relationship.

My therapy lasted six weeks. The time frame was Kay's suggestion, as she sensed I was fearful of becoming dependent. Did she trust I would seek additional therapy when I was ready to see more? When we were done, I told Kay I wanted to be her. She said I would need a doctorate. There ensued a frank conversation with my husband.

"Let me get this straight. You want to quit your career, live away from home for four years and get your doctorate?"

"Yes."

"Okay. I'm in."

That fall I went from having a parking space and a secretary to a dorm room at the University of Georgia and a roommate 21 years my junior. On the first day of class I remember excitedly telling the cleaning lady I was staying in the same dorm I'd been in as a freshman more than 20 years earlier. Incredulous, she asked: "Ain't you graduated yet?"

At 41 I was the oldest member of my cohort. My major professor told me the following year the admissions committee decided to admit only younger candidates—something about their being more malleable, I heard. Had I applied a year later I would have been passed over. This felt like the second divine intervention on my way to becoming a therapist, the first being when I traded my reactivity for the opportunity to have Kay Shurden as my therapist.

When I began the clinical portion of the program, my first assigned clients were a lesbian couple who, to this day, I credit with my early fascination with couples' work and sexuality. They were dream clients because they both wanted the relationship to heal and worked hard toward that end. Happy with their outcome, they told their community. Soon my fellow clinicians dubbed me the "gay therapist." I am forever grateful that these first clients forgave my inexperience. I recall one replying, when I made what I thought was an astute observation, "No shit, Sherlock." I had yet to learn it was about them, not me. These ladies provided me an introduction to couples' work and an education I would otherwise have missed.

While my preference remained steadfast for the more insight-oriented theoretical models throughout my program, I was to learn much from a supervisor who was a Brief Therapy advocate. He experimented with "the bug in the ear," whereby he could communicate with clinicians from behind the mirror via a small wireless microphone in the therapist's ear. Trying to attend to both clients and supervisor simultaneously was a little disconcerting. Once I gave a recommendation to a couple only to receive an immediate directive from my supervisor to do just the opposite. My next comment began with, "On the other hand…"

My supervision partner was bolder. When he tired of interruptions and suggestions that he felt were unhelpful, he turned off his microphone. Though often reproved for his impudence, he provided much comic relief in both individual and group supervision. My biggest takeaway from Brief Therapy was when to use it. When a client told me," I don't want to know how I got here; I just want to resolve this problem," it came in handy.

Four years later as I walked across the stage to receive my diploma I thought, "Wait, I don't know enough." This time it was an astute observation. Over the next 21 years, I was to learn that formal education gives one credentials, but therapy is learned on the job.

Back home, my family gathered to celebrate. A son-in-law appeared to be having a difficult time, so I pulled him aside to see what was bothering him. He asked if people walked into a room with me, sat down and talked for a while, and then I took money from them. My explanation that there was a little more to it did not suffice. He shook his head and walked away. He made me think of the "imposter syndrome"—which suggests that some of us are waiting for the other shoe to fall—meaning the world will find out we are not all we claim to be. Maybe my son-in-law was on to me.

I joined the faculty of Mercer's Marriage and Family Therapy Program in 1993. My former therapist was now my colleague. Within a short time, our program was adopted by Mercer's medical school, bringing opportunities for collaboration with family physicians and psychiatrists. I came to appreciate the practice of Medical Family Therapy; especially how acute and chronic illnesses impact couples. This model considers individuals' family systems along with their physical, mental, and spiritual health in addition to their relationships with health care providers. The overall goal is to increase the client's ability to deal with life's hurdles surrounding illness, while fostering the ability to communicate effectively with loved ones and members of the health care system.

I learned the hard way not to make a cold call to a client's physician. My first attempt was to a busy doctor who was kind enough to take my call but asked, "Why are you calling me?" After that I wrote short letters outlining clients' goals and sometimes progress updates, and these were far better received.

Later I practiced Equine Assisted Psychotherapy as part of a research project. EAP involves a therapist, a horse, a horse specialist, and one or more clients. All the work is done on the ground, with the horse specialist accessing the temperament and readiness of the horse before work begins and also monitoring for safety throughout the session. During my training I learned it can take a very short time to get to the crux of a couple's issues by putting them in an arena with a horse and directing them to halter and saddle the horse using only nonverbal communication. Patterns of interaction and problems with communication emerge within minutes.

A good illustration of how quickly issues surface in EAP is the story of a therapist and an angry adolescent. The client was instructed to catch and halter the horse. As she approached the horse, she jumped back.

The therapist asked, "What just happened?"

"The horse tried to kick me!"

"Interesting."

Instructed to approach the horse a second time, the adolescent again jumped back.

"What just happened?"

"The horse tried to bite me!"

"Interesting."

On the client's third attempt, the horse sat down with his legs splayed out.

"What just happened?"

"The horse sat on its ass to show me I'm being an ass."

"Interesting."

Did this actually happen? No, horses rest one leg at a time while standing. But the story is a staple for therapy sessions. Working with horses helped me be a better therapist. Horses never lie; they are honest with their emotions and can ferret out deception like a polygraph. They like leadership. When no one is in charge, they will step up to fill the void. They can be kind. When a horse goes blind, another horse will become his "buddy" and lead him to the food trough at feed time. Being honest, kind, and providing leadership work equally well in the arena and the therapy room.

My Mercer family supported me when my husband died in December 2000. People remembered him fondly and referred to me as his wife for many years. My favorite was a lady who asked if I were Bill Powell's "widder." I was, and it was an honor. At the same time, I needed a chance to start over. In 2010, I transferred to Mercer's Atlanta MFT Program.

Practicing in midtown Atlanta brought a myriad of opportunities for working with couples. It kept me humble. There were failures as well as success. One of my first couples asked if they could rent me for the whole day. Their rationale was that they wanted to solve their problems quickly and get on with their lives. They left disappointed, not really understanding that the time between appointments is helpful for processing and growth.

The most memorable couple I could not help was two psychiatrists married to one another. They were intelligent, articulate, and skilled therapists themselves. Not a little intimidated, I used all my wares but could not influence the family system. It felt wrong to keep taking their money. When the wife asked if I would be willing to go back to school, I knew it was time to refer them on. I told them I had done everything I knew to do and that another therapist could surely serve them better. My fantasy is that they found the perfect therapist who may have helped them to save their marriage.

The couple who still makes me smile started off with the husband seeking individual therapy. He was in his 80s and had had a predilection for being spanked all his adult life. He was ashamed to tell his wife of his desire, leaving him to seek out prostitutes or forego gratification. He hesitatingly agreed to ask his wife to join us. This remarkable woman, also in her 80s, listened without judgment and herself suggested her husband permit her to spank him. This, she reasoned, would allow her to take part in meeting his needs—which would please her while she pleased him. And that's what they did. Sometime later they let me know it was still working.

Hearing peoples' stories never gets old. Learning how they love, who they grieve, what they're willing to die for literally and figuratively is a privilege. I remember liking most of them and when I didn't, I found something to value about their lives or their persons. I will never forget one lady's gleeful declaration when I asked what she did when she and her husband disagreed.

"I jump on his back and ride him like a horse!"

"Whoa," I offered.

"Ha!" she countered.

I found her spunky. At our last session she handed me a riding crop, "For your riding pleasure," she beamed.

For many clients, hypnosis proved to be a powerful tool. Hypnosis is relaxation and cooperation. It allows the client to circumvent the conscious mind (which is more prone to judgement and criticism) and to access the unconscious mind (which is more open to suggestion). I used hypnosis most often to alleviate anxiety and compulsive behaviors.

I began sessions by getting a description of the kind of place clients would go to feel relaxed and peaceful. With their eyes closed and following progressive relaxation, starting at the top of the head and warming the body to the soles of the feet, I would guide clients in a downward motion via the image of an escalator or a drifting boat until they arrived at a place where "Everything is as it should be." I described their peaceful place in inviting detail. While relaxing in this setting, I gave them both directives and indirect suggestions through stories—as some clients preferred straight talk and others learned best from tales seemingly about others. I would assist clients in slowly reacclimating to the present and then tell them, "Everything you need to know will go with you as you leave today." We did not discuss the hypnosis segment of the session afterwards.

Sometimes I gave a stone or other small talisman at the end of the session. One of my favorite medical students received a tiny doll. She told me she carried it with her and set it before her as she took her board exams. Focusing on the doll, she felt less anxious, and, after a few moments of progressive relaxation, she aced the exam.

Hypnosis is not a panacea, nor does it work with everyone. One couple who initially came for marital therapy was devastated when the wife was diagnosed with terminal cancer. She died during their course of treatment. The grieving husband was in shock. He was vulnerable and lonely. When he told me his widowed neighbor was a delightful woman and he was thinking about remarrying, I utilized hypnosis to give him permission to slow him down a bit. They were married in six weeks. He returned to therapy right away when he and his bride began to tangle. His new wife joined us, and together they responded to more traditional therapy.

One particularly sacred tenet that therapists uphold is that we must make sure our own houses are in order. Inevitably patients' issues resonate with us or trigger unfinished business, sending us back into therapy ourselves. When this occurred in my practice, I sought help for sibling incest.

In my late 20s my family gathered for Christmas at my older brother's townhome. Housed on the third floor, I awoke the first morning to find my brother sitting on the end of my bed. He asked if he could watch me masturbate. Using choice words, I invited him to leave.

A short time later I was in the shower when he let himself in the bathroom. I told him he had 1.5 seconds to leave before I started screaming. He made the deadline.

While he didn't actually touch me, I experienced shame and guilt. I told no one at the time, wondering if I were somehow responsible. There were other similar incidents that led to cutting off contact with my brother rather than facing the issue of being sexually pursued by my sibling and the ramifications for both my personal and professional life.

Many hours of therapy later I had done a fair but incomplete job of forgiving him. It was clear I was not finished because I still wanted an apology. Knowing better, I called my brother and asked for an apology or at least an acknowledgement that he had hurt me. He said, "That would be problematic." I left it that if he changed his mind to give me a call.

My therapist helped me let go of the notion that one day my brother would call and say what I wanted to hear. He helped me understand I could forgive my brother and not necessarily wish to have a relationship with him. Perhaps most importantly, my therapist helped me forgive myself and stop feeling responsible for another's behavior. My brother does not owe me an apology. Would it be nice if he did? Sure. But I am no longer waiting for that call.

Admittedly I am not a chef, but I can follow a recipe. I used one for therapy, learned from my therapists and from colleagues I admire. It calls for roughly three parts listening, two parts understanding, one part support, and a half-part loving confrontation. The latter is delivered sparingly, and timing is essential, the object being to confront old patterns in a loving way when a client is ready for change. Listening involves encouraging expression of all a client's parts, the likable and the not-so-pretty. Making it safe to be vulnerable is the heart of therapy. Understanding occurs when the client says or indicates, "You get me." Support includes the shared belief in the client's ability to change and the willingness to respect the client's pace. The measurements may vary depending on the client, but the basic recipe seemed to work. I hope my clients felt heard, understood, supported, and lovingly challenged in the therapy room with me. Some said they did.

Carl Jung subscribed to the notion that in life you choose a building, put your ladder against it, and climb up. Should you get to the top and discover your ladder is against the wrong building, you climb down and move your ladder. As a therapist, I liked my willingness to jump in the pool. When what I did was not working, I got out of the pool and found another. Taking risks while balancing the desire for adventure with the need for continuity was a path that worked.

Several years into retirement, I occasionally respond to friends and family who request an opinion. Most often it is to consider therapy to address not only the current problem but also to glean understanding of themselves and the dynamics that govern their relationships. We all have much to learn, which Albert Einstein spoke to when he wrote, "The pursuit of truth and beauty is a sphere of activity in which we are permitted to remain children all our lives."

In the movie, *Oh, God!* starring George Burns, even God was portrayed as having a learning curve. He shared that he made avocado pits too big and needed to spend more time with the animals. I'm good with avocado pits, but I totally agree about the animals. Spending time with them just makes sense. I do this every day every chance I get.

I try to live mostly in the present with an appreciation of the past and hope for the future. My clients gave me an opportunity to make a contribution, and former colleagues have become friends. I remain happiest when I can be of service in most any capacity. The words of Dag Hammarskjöld provide a scaffold for growth: "If only I may grow firmer, simpler, quieter, warmer." And of course, on occasion, rise up and sing and dance.

Seeing Things Differently

Kay Wilson Shurden

I moved to beautiful East Tennessee in 1969 to teach at Carson-Newman College in Jefferson City. Having taught in public schools and acquired a master's degree in English, I taught education courses and supervised English student teachers. In 1973 the college granted me a study leave, and I began working on a doctorate in education at the University of Tennessee in Knoxville, 30 miles from my home.

I was in a graduate class in educational psychology when my career path began to change. The professor was Dr. Sharon Lord, an unapologetic feminist, who spoke eloquently and passionately about the role of women in society. Betty Friedan had recently published her bellwether book, *The Feminine Mystique*. Feminism had begun to flourish in the South.

One particular day, Dr. Lord captured my attention and imagination. The subject for the class was "the stages of social development," especially of adolescents. She cited study after study that showed how culture shaped young boys and young girls differently. The studies demonstrated that societal norms and expectations conditioned boys to focus on their dreams, while adolescent girls were conditioned to focus on being attractive to boys. Society expected girls to attach themselves to someone who would give them status and love. The image was clear: boys drove, and girls rode in the passenger seat. The trick for girls was to find a boy who drove well and drove far.

Society's message to girls was clear: You are not to be too smart or too outspoken. You are to be as pretty as possible and find a boy who will be your ticket into life. Your own potential and dreams and challenge to unjust systems of society are not subjects for your consideration. Girls' value lay in their looks and non-challenging behavior.

I realized I had drunk the Kool-Aid! I grew up in the Delta of Mississippi in the 1950s and learned the compliance lesson well. I had chosen a career in teaching because it supplemented and didn't hinder the career of my husband. I pursued his dream with him instead.

I became very interested in how girls were conditioned to defer or even ignore their dreams. I developed my doctoral dissertation on the subject of how characters in literature tend to lower expectations for girls. Because readers identify with characters in books they read, I researched the books most commonly read by teenagers in America. Sure enough, the female characters in those books were mere bystanders, not actors or achievers. Female characters were on the sidelines, cheering the exploits and achievements of boys. The one character who was an exception was Scarlet O'Hara in *Gone with the Wind*. If you remember that novel, you know that the conniving Scarlet was not the best model of female achievement!

When I graduated with my Ed.D. and returned to supervising English student teachers from Carson-Newman College, most of whom were female, I found that I wasn't so much interested in their teaching skills as in their relationships and dreams for the future. I asked them: "Is teaching English your passion? Is teaching your dream? What sets you on fire? Are you of equal importance in your relationships?"

Following the completion of my degree at the University of Tennessee, I moved with my family to Louisville, Kentucky, where I hoped to secure a position with the education faculty at the University of Louisville. That was not to be. I was crushed to find out the position I wanted had been filled by someone else. I had to settle for teaching English at Shelby County High School nearby. We had three children approaching college age, and our family needed the additional income. However, I had formed a desire during my time at UT of helping women consider their dreams as important as their partners' dreams. How would I fulfill my dream?

I found an outlet for my dream of helping women make fulfilling choices by teaching an evening course called "New Horizons for

Women" at Bellarmine College in Louisville. The students, mostly middle-aged women who had raised their children, now were deciding what to do with the rest of their lives. They were excited to consider all the options. I gave them interest inventories and skill tests that helped reveal their potential. However, when many of them talked about their plans with their husbands, they were shocked to find out the men weren't too excited. Husbands asked questions such as: "That's all well and good, but who will pick up my shirts at the laundry?" or "Who will fix dinner?" The women were angry because they thought their turn had come. They wondered whether they could have their dreams and their marriages too. Would they have to settle for less in order to keep the peace?

At this juncture in 1978, Dr. Wayne Oates entered my life. He was a guest speaker in my husband's seminary class, and I joined them at lunch. Dr. Oates was an esteemed pastoral counselor who had recently become a diplomate in the exciting new field of marriage and family therapy. I had never heard of that field. When I told Dr. Oates about my students' predicament of feeling they must choose between their marriages and their careers, he invited me to work with him and become certified as a family therapist. I accepted.

Dr. Oates explained that the marriage and family therapy field originated when men returned from World War II and found women in both the workplace and at home taking leadership roles. Conflict ensued. Most therapy at the time was done on an individual basis, so no one was equipped to deal with the conflict within established relationships. Dr. Murray Bowen, a psychiatrist, developed a way of helping reduce family conflict and promoting fairness. He called it the Family Systems model of therapy.

Dr. Bowen saw the family system much like systems in the natural world. Systems impose roles and expectations on their members. Systems also resist change. But Bowen insisted that change can occur when families discuss situations openly. The family system can endure as long as family members accommodate to each other's needs.

I came to see that the role of the therapist is to support the changing needs of family members so the family system can continue in a fair manner for all. Change was possible if the therapist supported the family as the members learned new roles. The family system could accommodate new roles for women.

I worked from 1980 to 1982 at General Hospital in Louisville under the supervision of Dr. Oates and earned certification as a family therapist. In 1983 my husband and I moved to Mercer University in Macon, Georgia, where I joined the faculty at the new Mercer Medical School. Established to serve rural Georgia, the founders of the medical school had adopted a bio-psycho-social model of health and illness. They therefore needed therapists to co-teach medical students with physicians. Mercer helped birth an exciting new field of Family Systems Medicine.

During my first year at the medical school a colleague, Mary Anne Armour, and I designed and established a master's degree program in family therapy. We wanted to teach therapists to do the important work needed to keep families together while they negotiated change.

At the same time that I was teaching medical school students how powerful Family Systems can be in supporting health and reducing illness, I also was teaching classes in Family Systems to therapy students. In addition, I started a therapy practice in the clinic at the medical school where I worked with families, couples, and individuals. I soon discovered it was easier to teach the *theory* of change than to *practice* it! How difficult change can be! Every change brings about the loss of something familiar and a sense of security.

I also learned that the therapist herself often needs therapy. I entered my own therapy several times while all these changes were taking place in my life. Our three children had left home, and I had gone from supervising English student teachers, to wanting to help women find their dreams, to helping families adjust to changing roles and rules. I realized in therapy that I carried the rules I learned in my first family with me into adulthood. I had learned early to be a people-pleaser. I had to begin to learn to say, "I see things differently" and find my own voice. This was and still is a learning process. Even desired change is not easy!

I taught at Mercer Medical School for 17 years before retiring in 2000. After I retired, I had a small practice in an office in my home. I also enjoyed several other activities: teaching the Enneagram, teaching about systems, and leading workshops on women's issues. I have even enjoyed writing this chapter for a book edited by one of my former students.

In conducting therapy, first and most important, *I listened.* I considered the therapy hour to be a time and place for clients to talk. They wanted to be heard, not analyzed nor directed. They wanted the attentive ear of someone who cared and wanted to help. I became a safe harbor at which they could dock. I listened carefully to what they had to say. I noted tears and anger and sighs and words. I kept quiet and listened.

I *invited.* If clients discussed a troubled relationship, I invited them to bring the person with them to a future session. I knew I would benefit from hearing a different perspective on the issue. If the problem was a family one, I invited the whole family to come. I wanted each family member present to voice their point of view.

I *questioned.* I asked: "What do you want to change?" "What have you tried that hasn't worked?" "Who is your support system? "What did you learn was important in the family you grew up in?" "How do you think I can help?" I considered my job as a therapist was to enable the client to discover the answer to their own problems with support from me. I did not consider it was my job to "fix" them or become the parent who told them what to do. Sometimes I asked them, "If a dear friend or family member came to you with this same situation, what would you advise that person to do?" Often, they saw a path forward from this line of questioning.

I *suggested.* Sometimes I asked clients to take a small deliberate action before our next meeting. Doing something only a little different can change one's "dance" with others. Patterns can change when someone refuses to respond or act in their regular way. I wanted them to see how much they were part of the pattern they wished to change. Systems of relationship, I am convinced, change with small steps.

I *introduced.* I often suggested that clients take an Enneagram test. The Enneagram is a personality typology that describes the strengths and weaknesses of different ways of interacting with others. Someone can be helped to see that although their personality is different from others, they can appreciate the strengths and weaknesses in themselves and the others in their life. Since we can only change ourselves—not another person—doing less or more of a characteristic way of behaving can bring a change in relationships. (This Enneagram has been very helpful to me in understanding myself and others in my life. I suggested it as a tool of self-understanding where I thought it was appropriate.)

I *taught.* Being a teacher, I taught! I commented about the expectations of the larger culture for women and men. This was a way of challenging cultural restrictions that kept clients from moving forward in their lives. I hoped that by seeing problems as challenges, they would have more energy and imagination to see their way forward. Problems can, I think, appear unsolvable and heavy. Challenges call us to imagine a better, fairer future. I often suggested books and poetry that had relevance to their quest for direction. I kept copies of Mary Oliver's poem "The Journey" to give to clients so they could see past a particular tough situation. Oliver said that no matter how loud and insistent the voices around you are, you need to rely on your own deep needs and dreams on the journey of life.

I have a master's degree in English literature from a former life, and I have always enjoyed reading novels. In therapy I saw each client who walked through the door to my therapy room as a great novel I was privileged to read. But therapy was more than that to me. I saw therapy as a birthing place for a richer, more connected life for the client and for myself.

My Name and Legacy

Andrea Meyer Stinson

My journey to becoming a therapist occurred over many years and included nudges from friends, family, and a legacy from the past. From early childhood experiences, to family-of-origin narratives, I was destined to become a family therapist and a systemic thinker.

My childhood was fraught with anxiety and worry. I was a shy and introverted child, who often complained of headaches and stomach aches. I was too scared to order meals at a restaurant by myself. In third grade it became worse, and I was afraid of attending school and spending the night at friends' homes. One day I called from school, saying to my mother I was sick and needed to come home. She encouraged me lovingly to stay and that I would be fine. I told her, "If you don't pick me up, I won't love you anymore!" Soon after this incident (from my childhood memory) we attended therapy. I remember vividly meeting with a family therapist, who had my parents and siblings all together in one room. At the time I had no clue what was happening. We played some games and talked to the therapist. I only remember the one session. Now looking back, I think the therapist was trying to expand the system in therapy and see what was influencing my anxiety and worry. I can see now that this was my first introduction into a family systems approach to psychotherapy.

I was named for my maternal grandmother, Catherine SeLaine Folk. I never met my grandmother, as she died from cirrhosis of the liver when my mother was 13. I know very little about my grandmother, but from an early age I knew that she died from drinking. I've always felt my grandmother's presence in my life, which is hard to explain since I've never known her. My mother has rarely shared memories of her mother and when asked has few things to say about her. It's been hard to gain a clear picture of who my grandmother was and her personality. In reading between the lines, it appears that my maternal grandfather was also a problematic drinker. My mother was allowed to get her driver's license at an early age and became responsible for the household tasks, such as grocery shopping and cooking. My mother was not told about her mother's illness nor the likelihood that she would die, but she was sent to another state to "visit" with a friend for the summer. The next thing she remembers, she was called back to her mother's bedside. Her mother was in a coma and soon after died. My mother had no opportunity to say goodbye or understand what happened. This began a legacy that I believe still influences me today.

As I grew older, I learned how to manage my anxiety and worry. I remember times when I would wake up in the night and tell my mom that my "brain was confused and had too many thoughts." She would give me hot chocolate, and it would help me get back to sleep. I didn't know what was happening, but later I realized that it was childhood anxiety. My mother is a very anxious person. She was always present physically in my childhood, but I could sense that her mind was consumed. She was thinking of a thousand other things at the same time. My father traveled a lot for his job, but at home he was jovial, fun, and loving. My parents are very different people who met and married when my mother was 18 years old and had their first child the next year. They remain married to this day and have learned to live with each other's quirks and personality differences.

High school was a pivotal point in my development as a person and future therapist. I continued to experience anxiety and depression. I was acutely aware of others' emotions and was a people-pleaser. I often struggled to decide what I wanted for myself. These are personal traits that led to my career as a family therapist but also created challenges in my personal life. Throughout high school I became interested in helping others who were new or needed support at my school. I joined two groups that were my first exposure to the possibility of becoming a therapist: peer leaders and peer support group facilitation. As a peer leader, I welcomed and mentored new students at school. As a peer support group facilitator, I met monthly with a group of peers to share our struggles and encourage one another to talk and share. In these two roles I was first introduced to the concepts of mental health and wellness.

Despite these amazing experiences, my anxiety and depression became problematic in my senior year of high school. I experienced a difficult romantic relationship, and this spiraled into thoughts of self-harm and suicide. A good friend told my parents of the thoughts, and I was immediately taken to a therapist. My therapist, Ms. Laura, helped me to see that I had more power and could make decisions for myself—not just for others. I quit several teams and activities and started on medication. Meeting with the psychiatrist and sharing my thoughts of self-harm in front of my parents was a difficult memory of this time. Slowly and with the support from a therapist and my friends/family, I emerged from this dark time with a new sense of self and future.

Although depression left me that year, anxiety has been a constant companion throughout my life. Anxiety reared its ugly head again as I was figuring out my options after undergraduate school. I had luckily landed in a Psychology of Relationships class at the University of Georgia as a sophomore, and I knew immediately that I wanted to pursue a degree that led to working with people. Coming from a family of engineers, it was difficult to explain this career path to my parents and siblings. In my junior year, however, I enrolled in a special seminar in couples' therapy. At that same time, I found a way to earn internship hours in the couple and family therapy clinic. With exposure to this kind of therapy, along with guidance from graduate students and professors, I found a path forward in pursuing a master's degree in marriage and family therapy. Despite this discovery, anxiety took over my life. After experiencing my first anxiety/panic attack, I sought therapy again at the psychology clinic at UGA. I learned to manage my anxiety with help from a therapist and hard work.

As I began to emerge as an adult and to differentiate from my family of origin, I made several realizations during college. It became more and more clear to me that my parents had a problematic relationship with drinking. I would call my mother at night to share something, but the next morning she would not remember what we had talked about on the phone. I also noticed when I visited home that she had a cooler in her room with alcoholic beverages. As a petite woman, she could drink more than most adult men! My father would fluctuate between drinking with my mother and then deciding to stop and be completely alcohol-free. During times of not drinking, he would call me and ask how to manage my mother's drinking. I was experiencing increasing levels of triangulation in my parent's relationship! Little did I know that the anxiety I was experiencing in college was being influenced by my family-of-origin interactions. My therapist at the psychology clinic, because of her individual approach to therapy, did not ask about these influences. From a Bowenian perspective, I was learning how to balance togetherness and separateness with my parents—along with a strong destructive entitlement!

I pursued training in marriage and family therapy at Purdue University in northwest Indiana. It was my first time living away from my family and with a partner. I fully immersed myself in learning the craft of therapy, while also building lifelong friendships with my peers. I graduated and found my first job as a therapist in a residential and day treatment program. The on-the-job training was intense! I had the theoretical and practical foundations, but I soon realized it was much different in the community setting. Over a few years of working with severe mental health issues in children and families, I made the decision to begin a doctoral program. I knew that only practicing as a therapist was not how I saw my future; rather I wanted to be able to teach, supervise, and mentor new therapists. I found the right fit at the MFT program at Florida State University. While there, I honed my therapy skills and became a solid researcher. With these experiences I was lucky to find a position back in Georgia at Mercer University, where I have been ever since.

As is often the case in life, while my educational and academic pursuits were flourishing, my personal life was in turmoil. I had married and tried to start a family with my college sweetheart. We were devastated to learn that we had infertility. For more than five years we tried to grow our family, using all medical means possible. Many large and small losses occurred, including several miscarriages. These wounds severely impacted our relationship, which didn't become evident until a few years later. Once we moved to Macon, we made the decision to adopt. We became foster parents and then adopted our daughter.

Becoming a parent and mother has been the most transformative and challenging part of my life, and it has permanently changed me as a therapist. Unfortunately, the old wounds were too much to bear and led to the dissolving of my marriage. Being a therapist while going through a divorce is not something I would recommend. It made me doubt everything about myself and my choices in life. Through additional therapy and support from family and friends, however, I realized that tough decisions are often needed. Brene Brown writes that "the most powerful teaching moments are those where you screw up." I wholeheartedly believe in this mantra as both a person and a therapist! Since this time of pain and suffering, I have met and married my new partner and found true relational healing. I've also been blessed with another child. The world works in mysterious and mystical ways....

The elements that influence my approach to therapy come from my personal and family-of-origin experiences. I also feel strongly that my responsibility as a therapist is to understand and adapt to the approach that is best for my clients. I start all therapy sessions with two primary goals: 1) to ensure the clients feel understood and safe and 2) to understand the language they use to describe the problems and potential solutions in their lives.

My influences are many and have varied over time, especially as I have gained experience in a variety of clinical settings. Early on in my career I strongly gravitated toward solution-focused therapy. I was fascinated by the idea that the problems in our lives are not the real problem; rather, the way we talk about them and the language we use is the problem. In a similar vein, narrative therapy and especially the concept of externalizing problems has been very helpful. For many people externalizing offers freedom, hope, and the potential for a new way of looking at themselves and others. While in a training clinic, I found the freedom and ability to use postmodern and language-oriented approaches with most of my clients.

As I began working in the residential and day treatment setting, the postmodern approaches were more difficult to apply. I found myself drawn to more modern perspectives and psychoeducation, such as structural family therapy and cognitive behavioral therapy. At the time I was overwhelmed with the severity of the child/family symptoms and struggled to understand the level of trauma and toxic stress experienced by most of my clients. I had my first experience with home visits, which became such an eye-opening and challenging part of my education as a therapist. Up to this point in my career I did not have to face my many privileges as a white, cisgender, heterosexual woman from a socioeconomically advantaged background. I saw firsthand what poverty and intergenerational trauma can do to a family and to parent-child relationships. Through these clinical years I learned that context and social factors play a much larger role in families than what is often acknowledged in family therapy models and in the therapy room.

As I returned to a more academic clinical setting, I was allowed again to experiment and practice my systemic therapy approach. I gained experience in working in a therapeutic supervised visitation program, which opened my eyes to the essential nature of early childhood experiences and infant mental health. I also worked as an in-home family therapist to foster children and families, where I expanded into family play and individual play therapy. I came to realize more and more the importance of experience and emotion in the therapy space. I was drawn to additional approaches that focused on creating new attachment relationships and building connections to health relationships.

Since working in an academic setting at Mercer, I have enjoyed revisiting all the major therapeutic models of MFT/systemic practice and enjoy teaching them to my students. When I reread the works of Bowden, Satir, Minuchin, and others I see it through a new light given the variety of clinical experiences I've had. Two recent experiences led me to focus more on parent-child relationships, learning about parent-child interaction therapy and perinatal mood and anxiety disorders. I've also been privileged to expand my knowledge of interpersonal neuroscience and addressing the importance of resilience and toxic stress. Ultimately, I have held true to my systemic roots with a focus on attachment, emotional regulation, and building healing through corrective emotional experiences. I do this via the language and narratives that people tell themselves and others about their relationships.

For me, the most important element of practicing as a therapist is attunement, both within myself and between myself and my clients. Attuned interactions with others lead to health bonding and attachment. Becoming more comfortable with being my true self in the therapy room is key. This means I use humor, self-disclosure, and my own reflections on the emotional climate of the room to help clients move toward change in their relationships and overall lives. Health is not just the absence of symptoms; it is the presence of meaning, connections, and support with others. It is the ability to manage stress and cope with suffering—because it will occur in life—when necessary, adapting and overcoming via resilience. In the end, my hope is to offer clients the space and time to discover their own needs to achieve health and healing and to guide them toward ways of progressing to that preferred narrative and future.

In recent years I have become more interested in applying the ideas of systems theory outside of the therapy room. I have noticed a repeating pattern in my work with families and children, which often involved early childhood disruption or trauma, along with toxic stress, and therefore impaired parent-child relationships. Early in my career, I often reflected that it was the parent's responsibility to achieve this type of attuned and healthy relationship with their child, no matter their previous experiences or current situations. Now I better understand that individuals are impacted by the larger systems and experiences around them. This includes economic, social, and spiritual components. It also acknowledges that powerful forces such as racism, sexism, and heterosexism (among many others) can impact the narratives and stories we tell ourselves. It can also limit the access to resources and power that many people in privileged positions have. This realization has led to my work in larger communities to address the impact of adversity, toxic stress, and trauma on developing children and families. By building a common language and collaboration across groups that work with children and families, we can help prevent or identify these situations early on in life and to build accessible and culturally relevant supports for parents and caregivers. To see this happen in the therapy room, systemic therapists must get engaged and advocate for larger changes at the society and policy level. We must advocate for our clients!

Relationships shape who we are and what we become. The many relationships I've had in my life have been key to my development as a therapist. My parents, siblings, teachers, professors, mentors, and many others have nudged and helped me along this path. My students and clients have been important teachers too. The pain and suffering of infertility, miscarriage, and divorce broke me, but also allowed me to become healthier and to create a new sense of self. I must also acknowledge the legacy of my grandmother; her death and the impact it has had on my mother will always be a part of my story. In looking back, it now makes perfect sense why I feel so passionate about building connections and healing through relationships. I continue to be influenced by the loss and trauma experienced in my family of origin. I hope that I can continue to value and be open to new experiences on this lifelong journey of becoming a therapist.

My Journey into Therapy

Kerri S. Thompson

I took the long, winding, scenic route into work as a therapist. It was never my intention to work in this capacity. I believe my interest in others was fostered while growing up as an Army brat. I lived as far south as Atlanta, Georgia, as far north as West Point, New York, as far northwest as Indianapolis, Indiana, as far west as Houston, Texas, and as far east as Heidelberg, Germany, with several stints in Virginia and another in Maryland. We moved every three years or so. I found that each region had its own culture and way of doing things. It seemed there was no one right way of moving through life—there were many different ways to experience and appreciate others. While living in Germany, I had the distinct experience of being the other. We were guests in another nation, with a range of opinions of our presence. Our first language was not the primary language of the country. Holiday observances varied from our own. It was a rich, as well as humbling, experience.

I began thinking about working with people during college as a sociology major with a psychology minor at The College of William and Mary in Williamsburg, Virginia. I veered toward the classes that were experiential and allowed me to volunteer: one at a shelter for battered women and another at a nursing home. I felt drawn to justice-oriented work. As unlikely as this sounds, Dr. David Aday's criminology class, which discussed social order, organization and norms, and the treatment of those who find themselves in the margins of society—victims of domestic violence and violent crime, inmates in the prison system, people with mental illness, among others—was pivotal in my thinking of my place in the larger order of things. This class prompted my thoughts toward people outside of the mainstream.

Over the course of my senior year, I tried to envision what would be next after college. I saw myself working directly with people in need, but knew I needed further training or education *and* confidence to do so. I learned about an accredited school of social work at the Southern Baptist Theological Seminary in Louisville, Kentucky. I was drawn to the curriculum that first provided a theological foundation before introducing the social work courses. The theological coursework added a year to the usual two-year MSW program.

The program was built on the Family Systems Theory, in which an individual is viewed as a part of the larger family unit. Each member of the family impacts the well-being of the others in the family unit, thereby impacting the overall balance or equilibrium of the larger unit. The program culminated with an integrative project in which we considered how the theoretical knowledge gained in classes intersected with our faith and sense of calling, and how it all applied in practical ways in our internships. This framework made so much sense to me, connecting the mind and spirit to understand one's purpose and in one's work.

My first internship was in a homeless shelter where I did case management. The shelter was unique in that, rather than serving either women with children or men, it served families with children. This was the only shelter in the area that allowed women and men with children to stay together, rather than separating families. The next year I worked in the aging services for the Department of Community Services in Louisville. In that internship I was involved with a task force created from a coalition of community leaders and members in an initial phase of a larger project that addressed elder abuse in Jefferson County, Kentucky.

A thread that ran through college and grad school was the issue of abuse in varying forms—domestic abuse, child abuse, elder abuse. I thought my path would continue along these lines. However, directly after seminary I moved with my husband to Charlottesville, Virginia, where he began studies toward a Ph.D. at the University of Virginia. My career immediately detoured from the path I envisioned. I applied for any and every job, eventually getting a job working with adults with developmental disabilities. During my initial job search, I saw a social work position at the local hospice and was drawn to it right away. Something moved me in a way that none of the other jobs did. It seemed like the kind of work in which an approach connecting the mind, body, and spirit would be relevant and effective. I did not get the job initially, but I applied again just over a year later when I saw another position advertised. The second time I was hired as a social worker with Hospice of the Piedmont.

There is some irony to me working in a setting that serves people with terminal illnesses, as a person who felt faint at the sight of my toddler's first (barely) split lip. I generally don't handle physical injury well. There are times when terminal illnesses engage many of the senses with sights, smells, and sounds.

An early visit to a young man with very advanced mouth cancer challenged me to push through my queasiness and unease. His face was deformed with tumors that misshaped his mouth, tongue, and lips to the point that he could no longer close his mouth. He could not keep the saliva that mixed with blood from dripping from his mouth. The smell of cancer eating through his flesh was pungent. He had difficulty meeting my eyes. He sat hunched on the edge of the bed that had been set up in the front room of his brother's home, eyes fixed on the floor. I think he was aware of the odor and his appearance, neither of which he could control. However, I did not want to shrink away from him, thereby confirming the need for his self-consciousness. I remembered the adage that "the eyes are the windows to the soul," so that is where I sought to connect. Our eyes met for a few moments—I hoped to acknowledge his humanity and honor his dignity. My purpose in being there was to assess his needs and determine with him how the hospice team could best be of assistance. That was accomplished. But even more so, I hoped that he felt respected and seen. I was humbled and changed by our encounter. That experience set me on a course in which I realized, over and over again, that the work was not about me. It also expanded my compassion for those hurting and taught me that I possessed fortitude about which I was unaware.

Therapy was an unexpected career path for me, as I had ruled it out many years ago. A couple years into my hospice career and soon after I took the licensure exam, I was invited to join another LCSW and an LPC in their private practice. They were members of my church at the time and were respected clinicians in the community. I was completely caught off guard. The voice of self-doubt in my mind grew from whispers to shouts. I thought of all the reasons I was not suited, not prepared, or not experienced enough. I met with them, however, and heard about their practice and what it meant to them. It didn't feel like the right choice at that time, so I remained in hospice care another 18 years or so.

Later in life, upon reflection, I realized that my thoughts of self-doubt about "not being enough" to provide therapy joined other experiences over my lifetime in what I came to understand as social anxiety. There have been times that it has been paralyzing and rendered me silent. There have been countless situations that I shied away from because the overwhelming anxiety felt unyielding. I have reframed my social anxiety as a point of connection, however, and I add it to a variety of life experiences through which I relate to clients. I believe there are seasons of life, and at this point feel I have weathered many life events and changes that are relevant to others and that inform my work—in addition to book knowledge. My family has been my classroom on adoption, living in a multigenerational home, caregiving, death, grief, chronic illness, depression, anxiety, and social anxiety—to name a few. I try to meet clients where they are, and in some cases I have life experience from which to draw. I am careful about the use of self, transference, and countertransference in sessions. But I have a well of empathy I attribute to my life experiences and from which I draw.

My vision of my role as a therapist is informed by my decades in end-of-life care. As a social worker and bereavement coordinator for 20 cumulative years, I saw myself walking beside patients and families for just a part of their journey. I felt privileged to be invited along. I knew these were people who had lived full and vibrant lives prior to their need for hospice care. I only knew a small part of their story, though I often left someone's side appreciating what I learned and wanting to know more. I felt that I was bearing witness, in a way, to their experiences, hopes, sorrows, and pain. I worked intentionally to make them feel seen and heard. Hospice work is where I learned the importance of presence. When I am with clients, they are the most important thing to me in that moment. I attend with eye contact, facial expressions, and body language. I match their energy. I meet them where they are, but also challenge them when needed and introduce the possibility of change.

In my hospice work, the patient's goals became the team's goals. We worked toward the level of comfort they wished for—physical comfort, emotional comfort, spiritual comfort. This work often involved hard decisions, such as finding the right amount of medication to ease pain to a tolerable level while also allowing for enough alertness to still communicate with loved ones. My hope was to create a safe space in which they could voice feelings, process fears, reconcile when needed, and find a measure of peace. I learned that hope is important in living, as much as in dying.

In my therapy work, my clients' goals become my goals. Sometimes I frame goals as hopes. During clients' first appointment, I express my hope that the office or the time spent in session (if virtual) becomes safe space to talk about the things they need to talk about. I acknowledge that the act of reaching out for help is an act of strength, in and of itself, particularly if a client frames the need for help as weakness. I assure them that it takes courage to be vulnerable with a stranger; that I recognize the risk they are taking; that I appreciate their trust. Then we explore their hope in reaching out, what they want to accomplish, and where to start. My job is to hold the space so that it is safe to do the needed work.

David Kessler, a student of Elizabeth Kubler-Ross, recently named a sixth stage of dying as finding meaning. This is a valuable process of making sense of an experience or experiences at hand. I believe that we all have a story to tell. I want to hear my clients' stories. When working with terminally ill patients, I would often engage in life review, in which finding meaning occurs. This is a telling of one's experiences, relationships, goals met or missed, and regrets. It is a process of making sense of one's life. Often, therapy employs a similar process of finding the meaning of life experiences. I ask questions. I listen a lot. I identify clients' important events and the beliefs surrounding these that give them value. Sometimes I challenge negative thoughts. Other times I help reframe views to healthier versions of truth.

In hospice work, the family is considered the unit of care. A terminal illness impacts each family member individually and also the family as a whole. The same is true for the family of someone experiencing depression or anxiety. The family system is impacted by the individual's struggle, and the individual is impacted by the family system. One's family of origin offers a lot of information about history, values, shared beliefs, and so on. We all learn from the way we were raised as children, from the values we were taught, and from the relationships we observed. This is part of every client's story I want to hear. I want to help clients find meaning and connection in their experiences to help deepen their understanding of themselves, their place in the world, and what they believe is possible.

My Path to Career Integration

Betty Williams

I have worked as a marriage and family therapist, counselor, chaplain, ministerial coach, consultant, and spiritual director. These titles make up my 30-plus years as a career "people helper." The thread that runs through the titles and the career years is the academic preparation mixed with on-the-job training that happened intentionally and sometimes unintentionally. The degrees have mostly helped give language to the concepts, theories, principles, and interventions that come from a lifetime of learning. I loved my educational process from an undergraduate degree in English education to a master's in Family Systems to a doctorate in ministry with an emphasis in spirituality. However, more than the books—or at least just as much as the books—the students, professors, travels, institutions, and experiences shaped me into the therapist and person that I am today.

As a naïve 20-something, I managed to finish an education degree but didn't want to teach in the public school system. I got that far out of a desire "to change the world." I grew up in a large family in South Georgia (10 siblings). Being black and poor meant a lot of things, but it didn't mean there was an obvious door to success that was immediately apparent. The greatest things I had going for me as a graduate of a tiny high school in the middle of somewhere was a 4.0 academic average, a high school counselor who really liked me, relatives who were successful professional teachers, and a mentor who was a pastor of our small Baptist church. The latter had the most impact. My spirituality was a driving force for good. Despite the perilous potholes all around me—addiction, teenage pregnancy, legal problems, and violence—I was shown something pure, authentic, and good. Spiritual vision alongside the loving encouragement and role modeling of my pastor carried me through the years of discernment for purpose.

My first real job after attaining my four-year degree was as a group counselor for a religious nonprofit. The model for change for the agency was outdoor therapy with a positive peer culture curriculum. It was fairly new and innovative for the times. Insurance companies didn't easily jump on board with payment because the efficacy was probably still being researched and the interventions were at times spontaneous given the situation. Since I didn't have a psychology degree and had only one or two introductory psychology classes under my belt, when the experts would throw around terms such as *oppositional defiance, intermittently explosive, bipolar,* etc., I was clueless. However, I already had a lifetime of experience of learning how to calm anxieties in myself and others, mitigating wild conflict, and talking to people who were emotionally troubled. On top of that I was allowed to practice spiritual disciplines as a part of the everyday milieu of my 24-hour/3-day shift. I also leaned heavily on the curriculum I was taught and my very experienced colleagues who became like another family. By the time I left the agency I had been promoted to the administrative level, had seen more miracles than I could count, and knew that I needed more education in order to be more intentional about this "saving the world" business.

Interestingly enough, my next career move catapulted me back into the world of academia. The title of the job was admissions counselor at a small private university. The role included advising students about school choices that would lead to a career. I often interviewed students for college suitability, academic achievement, and leadership ability. The college offered scholarships for those fitting the appropriate categories. This was very different from my last job of working with very resistant clients who were at times threatening harm to self or others. That clientele was often disengaged from family, and the work was about re-connection. The students I met in high school gyms, offices, and cafeterias and in hotel conference rooms were mostly middle to upper middle class whose families were often or overly engaged with the process. Although this job was a transient one, I learned a great deal about presentation, connecting quickly with others, organization, and delivering extemporaneous speeches. Once again, what I had learned in the church setting helped my success in this arena. My pastoral mentor constantly pushed me to teach, preach, and sing. He believed that I was endowed with these specific gifts and admonished me to use them. When he traveled to different churches, I went with him and was often called on to do one of the three. I name the college admissions job as transient because of the brevity of my time in it and the fact that it led me to the next important chapter of my life. Being on that college campus was how I found out about the Marriage and Family Therapy Program. It was also the year that I made the transition from single life to married life.

I intuitively knew that the MFT program was the graduate program for me, mostly for the following reasons: My camp job helped me to fall in love with the idea of working with families to help them in getting to a healthier place. It also made me realize the unhealthiness of many families, not just my own. I really wanted to know what the research had to say about healthy families, because I had seen enough unhealthiness. Beginning my own marriage made this seem even more crucial. I looked at other programs, but the difference for me was the idea of family system theories. It also helped that one of the graduate admissions officers told me that this was one of the few programs at the time in which I would get almost immediate practicum experience. This really appealed to me because I learn best when I can immediately apply what I learn. After meeting the faculty, making friends with classmates, and starting my classes, I knew I was in the right place. I remember the first time I tried to explain a Bowen Systems theory concept to my husband. It didn't go over so well. He clearly set the boundary that at home I was a wife and not a therapist. This didn't stop me as a new student from "accidently" leaving books open to paragraphs that might be helpful to couples who were in our life-cycle stage. I have always believed in the integrity of practicing what I learn theoretically. It was a part of that whole "change the world" thing. I really believed—and still do— that if I am to teach someone a concept, I must at least believe in it enough to try it myself.

One of the greatest gifts of the MFT program was the increase in my emotional intelligence. By this I mean the classes, supervision, and the practicum work helped with self-assessment and the work of transformation. This graduate work changed my concept about "changing the world." Suddenly I knew that changing the world had to begin with changing me. I could then possibly influence people. I even liked that in this program we were called therapists and not counselors. The definition difference is subtle but helpful. The difference always reminded me that I had no control over whether anyone changed. My role was to offer an informed, refined presence that gave individuals and families the opportunity to instigate their change processes. This information totally informed my spirituality in a way that transformed my way of being in the world. I still believed in the idea of having impact but had the realization that I did not have to shoulder the responsibility. This was a good growth beginning that continued as I took on the huge role in the next major step in my journey. During and after the MFT program, I worked in a community service agency, a hospital, and several other nonprofits. The big move for me was going to work for a church. For years my heart longed to be in a world where I felt that my "spiritual gifts" would be given free reign. Working in a church allowed for this in ways I couldn't imagine possible. I don't think I could have grown the way I did in any other setting.

Indulge me while I describe the context. When I was hired the church had approximately 300 members. It had recently gone through a leadership change, so there were lots of changes happening quickly. Initially the church was approximately 20 percent black and 80 percent white, with a white lead pastor. When I left 15 years later, the church had grown to approximately 1,000 members with an interesting multicultural congregation that included internationals. I became the pastoral counselor with wide-ranging duties that included counseling congregational and community members. I also directed several departments, taught classes, developed curriculum, organized events, and spoke to groups on a regular basis. Everything I had done up to this point was great training for this huge role. There are two things I did while working there that will always hold a special place in my bag of life experiences. One was being a lead organizer for a conference in Yekaterinburg, Russia. This included partnering to organize a traveling team and raising the necessary funds. The other was organizing a benevolence trip to Monrovia, Liberia with a team of six black Americans. The fact that we were an entirely black team was highly unusual and maybe even a first to that particular African ministry.

These two events were so special to me because they allowed my counseling skills to be experienced on other continents. While in Russia—where I went more than once—not only was I speaking to groups through a translator, but I also remember speaking to women one-on-one about issues happening in their lives. Unlike doing counseling or social work in Georgia, I did not have names of resources for follow-up. I simply had the skills of presence, assessment, and possible coping interventions. Mostly, I started to become familiar with the value of spiritual disciplines and spiritual gifts. Understanding prayer and spiritual discernment became my greatest tools. Recognizing grace and supernatural intervention was crucial in not getting myself into trouble. The same was true in organizing and implementing the trip to Liberia. The goal of the team was to take needed supplies, medical help, and professional training to a small village on the outskirts of Monrovia. For me, the whole process included multiple layers of understanding about my family system culturally, a small bit about government systems, and a little more about religious systems. The nuances of what I learned about resiliency in the midst of great suffering is too much to recount here. However, I have to say that one of the great takeaways was learning about how psychological and spiritual interventions are often inherent in the human spirit. In the Liberian culture I found the interventions of song and dance to be most helpful. This was most evident in the village that seemed hundreds of miles from modern technology. The chanting, songs, and dancing provided evidence of generations of survival. For example, while some of the team who were medically trained helped a long line of people suffering from grave illness, we were being emotionally lifted in the middle of the village by music and free-form dancing. These experiences helped me to grow spiritually exponentially.

This was a major marker in what I consider integration of my self and my career. The master's level counselor training helped me to understand matters of the heart and head—emotions, thoughts, and behaviors that came from both. However, my work in the church gave me a hunger for learning more about matters of the spirit—the invisible connections with something much bigger than human physicality. Seminary seemed the right next step. At the master's degree level, I learned a great deal more about religious systems and the interaction of human beings within those systems. I thought this degree would lead me to a job that was right for me, but it wasn't exactly a linear path. I quickly realized that I was not meant to pastor a church. I enjoyed the work of chaplaincy. This role was an interesting integration of head, heart, and spirit work. The context of the work was prisons, hospitals, and hospices. Many of the issues were generally the same as in any other counseling context, but usually the clients were facing imminent crises. This made the focus of conversations more crucial and added the extra layer of longing for something bigger than the physical experience. Seeking to understand the spiritual journey of others was fascinating to me. The connection with clients that incorporated an awareness that something bigger than both of us was present seemed to bring more clarity to the encounter.

Once again, I was realizing that the impact for growth was often beyond education and at times beyond my understanding. The most impactful experiences for me were with those whose religious backgrounds were different from my own. The one that comes immediately to mind is the Muslim woman who had to challenge the local prison system in order to wear her religious head dress and attend services. I remember emotionally holding her through tearful conversations, advocating with the administration, and helping her connect to imams on the outside. An experience that was emotionally challenging for me involved a young, pregnant, self-avowed atheist who attended my spiritual direction groups held behind prison walls. After many meetings, we connected to the point that I was able to visit her while handcuffed to a hospital bed after her baby died. I prayed for her and tried to process grief with her without the ability to touch her and having to stand so many feet from her. After trying to hold her rage and grief for a few minutes, I said a tearful good-bye, knowing I would never see her again. There was also the Buddhist son that I sat with in a hospital waiting room while his father recovered from emergency surgery. In a few minutes of talking with him about his faith and coping skills, I gained incredible insight about Christianity. These stories along with many others led me back to seminary to seek more understanding.

My last educational experience included a research project that helped me with this idea of further integration of everything that I had done as a job and everything that I had learned both academically and experientially. My favorite part was the focus on spiritual direction. It meant going deeper into my own spiritual journey in order to impact my world. Still, I could not have been as proficient at this if I had not done the counseling training. Somewhere along the way I learned about compassion fatigue as a phenomenon that was affecting professional caregivers such as myself. This so resonated with me that I eventually decided to let this be the focus of my research project.

Once again, it seemed the perfect integration project. I would learn how professional caregivers build resiliency and focus on their spiritual coping skills. This time the context was a hospice, and the role was spiritual director. I spent weeks interviewing, documenting, analyzing, and synthesizing how medical professionals used the awareness of their spirituality to combat compassion fatigue. The end of the project included me doing one-to-one spiritual direction with a professional who scored highest on the compassion fatigue measuring instrument. The idea was to mitigate this professional's symptoms through the spiritual direction process. Looking back, an interesting unintended learning for me was having to be aware of when I was slipping into the role of counselor versus being a spiritual director. This awareness was incredibly freeing somehow. Although the skills involved overlap, there is very much a difference. Finishing this degree and project finally gave me peace about my professional role.

Over the years I had much consternation with myself about not settling into a career that had one title, consistent office hours, and a retirement package that would make me proud. It took me a long time to be "ok" with working out of purpose and not for the attainment of specific career goals. I would not be honest if I did not admit that I still sometimes struggle with this concept. However, for the most part I feel that the integration of head, heart, and spirit for me is this very thing. The roles of my career are just that—roles. They do not define my identity as I strive to impact the world. My ultimate goal is to leave the world a better place, starting with the people who are in my sphere of influence. When where I am working feels stagnant, counter-productive, or malignant, it is time for me to move on or to grow. I am very grateful for my training as a therapist. It serves as the backdrop for what I do in all of my roles.

An important part of integration is an awareness of how not to allow one role to usurp a role that you are being paid to perform. This has been one of the most important lessons of my life. Each role informs the other but shouldn't be confused when your client or company has contracted you to do a specific job. I try to make this clear in the beginning of any professional helping relationship. When or if I find myself slipping, I am intentional about correcting it. Accountability will always be needed and helps to enhance who we are and the impact we have. I will always be grateful and appreciative for the continued counsel, spiritual direction, and coaching that I receive.

Epilogue

I am not the girl I was when we gathered these clinicians to write this book. The world has changed and so have I in ways I did not want and could not have imagined. The current me wants to apologize to the patient women that have let me sulk and be sad, grieve and move slow.

For many months I had been unable to open the documents sent by writers and our editor. The girl that worked on the book during the height of the pandemic knew the book. She was settled and loved, had excitement overflowing about letting you read about these amazing women that have found their way to fulfilling work.

I am having to reach back and access that girl that worked with them and gathered their stories. She had plans to work and travel and rock in a rocking chair on her big wide open front porch that sits up high over the neighborhood where you can see people coming and going. We had plans. We called it Rock, Rock. This was what my husband Ross and I would say to each other rushing around looking for church socks or baseball uniform cleats. It was morning banter as we headed north for the commute to work or west to get the kids to school on time. Rock, Rock was the sound of the two rocking chairs on the front porch. The slow rock of the chairs was going to be our reward for making it through the busy years of our life together raising good kids. It was us, drinking hot coffee and talking about the wood bees, birds at the window feeder or the Sunday sermon. I imagined it slow and full of mostly true stories of our adventures that kept us so busy that we were often out of breath running around trying to get to these places. We would say, "Rock, Rock," and smile as we rushed away from each other doing what we had agreed was a rich life to review on that big porch.

The wife of Ross feels fragmented and struggles to tune in to that girl that was doing okay. It has been since March 2021 when he died of a heart attack at home.

Feeling fragmented is common when you experience a trauma. Our brains go to great lengths to help us manage and breathe and keep answering the phone when you would rather curl up in the fetal position in the corner of the room. I have been teaching about grief and trauma for several years now. Now I know to talk less. Listen more.

I am consolidating these fragmented parts each day to become thankful and hopeful. I am reaching for a place in life that is good and whole where I can give back some of what has been given to me. The pieces are coming together. More and more days are joyful, and it is true that it does get better.

From the moment of Ross' heart attack to this very minute I am writing this, I and my family have been cared for. We have been hugged, fed, listened to, sat with, laughed with, remembered the good and bad with and just 'loved up'. There is so much more that has been lavished on us and you know who you are, and I am thankful.

Barbara Newton

About the Editors

Barbara Ann Newton

Barbara Ann Newton calls Macon, Georgia, home. Born into an Air Force family they moved from base to base, every year, until high school. Following the family tradition she enlisted for 4 years of military service and went to college using her GI Bill. She completed her education at Mercer University with a master's degree in Marriage and Family Therapy. Barbara has practiced as a psychotherapist for 29 years. In her first book, she has knit together the experiences of an amazing community of women working as clinicians in diverse capacities. Their personal and professional stories and their passion for this work, have shaped many lives. Their unique paths and contributions are no longer the best kept secrets behind therapy doors. These colleagues and friends have found rich rewarding careers. Their desire to encourage growth within families and individuals is contagious, and the satisfaction from their work obvious in their stories.

Besides writing, Barbara likes spending time with family and friends, singing, attend the most incredible Baptist Church on the planet, traveling, sharing a meal with her besties and just having fun.

Kay Shurden

Dr. Kay Shurden has been a teacher for most of her adult life. She began by teaching Elementary School to help put her husband, Walter Shurden, through seminary. After gaining a Master's degree in English, she taught high school and college classes, which led to teaching in the Department of Education at Carson-Newman College in Jefferson City, TN.

After obtaining her Ed.D. from the University of Tennessee and being trained as a Marriage and Family Therapist, she joined the faculty of Mercer University School of Medicine in 1983. There she taught physicians in training how to work with patients and their families. While teaching medical students, she and a colleague developed a Master's program in Marriage and Family Therapy. She co-edited two books: WOMEN ON PILGRIMAGE, on challenges and changes in women's lives, and a book on vocation for young people, CALL WAITING. At present she is co-editing two books, one on women in ministry and one on women who became therapists.

The Shurdens have three grown children, six grandchildren, and a great grandson. Since being retired they enjoy visiting with family and friends, both those near and far away. They read all the books they didn't have time to read when they were working!

Kay Shurden has been honored by Baptist Women in Ministry as Churchwoman of the Year, by The Wayne Oates Institute as Outstanding Therapist, and by Crescent Hill Baptist Church, Louisville, KY and First Baptist Church of Christ, Macon, GA by her ordination as a deacon.

www.ingramcontent.com/pod-product-compliance
Lightning Source LLC
Chambersburg PA
CBHW060242030426

42335CB00014B/1575